Anyone looking to create powerful change in their lives and in the world must read this book."

Jerry McNeilly
High Ticket Closer
Charlotte, North Carolina

———

'The theme of this book is the most important element of success. Inspiration is essential. Try moving anyone, anything without an intense emotional connection is futile. The biggest mistake many make, that I have made, has been to set off on journeys of success without first identifying the inspiration; Or the reason behind why we're setting off in the first place.

Inspiration is the magnet of achievement. Robert Christiansen's book quantifies it. Inspiration, like any-thing else, can be discovered, learned and understood. This book is our guide.'

Greg McIntyre
McIntyre Elder Law
Shelby, North Carolina
www.mcintyreelderlaw.com

———

"As the director of an event venue and an entrepreneur, I engage with dozens of new people on a daily basis. What astounds me about Your Inspiration Is Needed is

how Rob blends his social theory research with a voice that moves me. I felt challenged to change how I saw the world through this accessible display of genuine anecdote, poignant history, and unyielding hope.

In a world of separation and despair, this is the book we've desperately needed."

Duncan Blount
Manager/Event Coordinator Uptown Indigo
Shelby NC, author and entrepreneur
www.uptownindigo.com

———

'Robert Christiansen's book is enlightening and thought-provoking. I found myself looking at things in a more creative and optimistic way. While being both inspirational and pragmatic, the author challenges you to look within, while giving practical strategies to do this. His view of inspiring others will help you develop life-long strategies to benefit those around you and, in doing so, change your own outlook on life for the better.

If you are willing to challenge your way of thinking, the way you view others and embrace a positive attitude, I highly recommend this book.'

Jane O'Keeffe
Student Support Coordinator
Northumbria University, UK

———

FRONT COVER DESIGN

It is not usual for an author to explain the image on the front cover of their book, but in this case I believe it will assist you to understand the why of it.

Most of us view a traditional world where monetary wealth, a great job, a beautiful big house, fancy cars, great health and a fabulous relationship are the ways to find happiness. This is the world 'out there' story.

But I believe by looking 'out there,' we are searching in the wrong direction. The world 'out there' is merely a reflection of the world within us. The true seat of power can only be found by looking within.

This is the reason I choose the front cover as a photographic negative. It represents the opposite, the reflection of what most people see as the real world.

The image is of the earth at night, the lights shining from the cityscapes below, and a web above with lights expanding brighter as more people focus within and find the connection to all things.

How your future develops is dependent on where you direct your awareness in this moment.

Will it be 'out there' or will it be within?

The front cover was designed by Debbie O'Byrne at Jetlaunch.

Endorsements for Your Inspiration is Needed

'An inspirational fresh voice in a field that can´t be stressed enough; for sake of humanity! Writing "from our midst", Robert Christiansen managed to shape a manual to "trigger the best in us". Guiding his readers through (seemingly) simple challenges, rather offering encouragement than doctrine, and not holding back in sharing his very own struggle in achieving the goal, he expounds a way of growing out of self-diminishing habits and insecurities in lifting others first.

Feasible to anyone, for one will detect oneself easily in his examples. So, dive in! Let`s shape a better world! Your Inspiration in Needed!'

Astrid Paul
General Practitioner, Holistic and Spiritual Medicine
Austria
www.holintmed.at

———

'Success in life should not be characterized by how much money we make, but by how we impact the lives of others. Your Inspiration is Needed hands you amazing insights into how we should be interacting with each other. This is the definitive book on successful behavior and living a successful life. I wish I had read it when I was younger.

'Robert Christiansen's Your Inspiration is Needed is a fine addition to the literature of personal growth and leadership development. It is so much more than a self-help or personal development guide. Through-out the book, Robert challenges us to claim our gifts and power and to lead by example. We are challenged to inspire our friends, neighbors, co-workers and institutions to be their best.

Finally, Your Inspiration is Needed asked us to recognize the very real connection of the personal to the planetary as we seek to create a just and sustainable future for all.'

Ron McCollum
MSW Social Worker/Educator/ Community
Collaborator
First Broad River Watershed Warrior

———

Thought-Provoking! Inspiring! Life-Changing!

Suzi Kennedy, RN, BS
Executive Director Life Enrichment Center,
Shelby NC
Lifeenrichmentcenter.org

———

'Your Inspiration is needed,' is thought provoking and challenging. Rob challenges us to get over ourselves to inspire others. He challenges us at the end of each

chapter through a 'challenge' which helps us implement change in our lives. This book is worth your time if you want to become a person who makes a difference, overcomes their own limitations to inspire, encourage and lift others in this journey of life.

Renee Bingham
Toastmaster Past Club President 2016-2017 and
Past Area Governor 2012-2013

———

'Robert Christiansen's Your Inspiration Is Needed, made me think about my relationships with others. I hadn't considered the effects a little support and encouragement have had on my life but on reflection its certainly helped me find direction. The book has prompted me to remember and where possible thank those that have given me inspiration. Reading this might just inspire some positive changes in all of us!'

Mark Archer
Restauranteur and Owner of Archers Restaurant
Chiang Mai, Thailand

———

"Rob's writing reminds me of the story of the Zen Master who ordered a hot dog and said, "make me one with everything." After handing the vendor the money, the monk asked about his change. "Change must come from within," the vendor stated. This book helps us on the

path to realizing that it is within all of us to create, change and inspire others and ourselves. We just have to look for it."

Jay Gragg CPA/ PFS
Shelby North Carolina USA
www.graggandgragg.com

———

'A fascinating and readable book, with great insight into the human psyche. It makes you stop and really think about the power that lies within us all.'

Laura Ashford
Horticulturist
Suffolk UK

———

'YOUR INSPIRATION IS NEEDED'

ROBERT CHRISTIANSEN

OTHER BOOKS BY THE AUTHOR

Rockstar Lawyer Co-authored with Greg McIntyre
Rockstar Business Co-authored with Greg McIntyre

Hans the Little Sailor. The oily engine
The Cosmic Adventures of Spaceman

This book is dedicated to those who seek change and hope to make a difference. Take nothing here as gospel. In his book 'The Ultimate Truth,' Lester Levenson said, "*Necessary is the proof of truth… Nothing should be accepted on hearsay. One should listen to, reflect upon, and then prove.*" Realize, what is in this book is how *I* see things. I advise you to read, reflect upon, discuss and prove before accepting anything.

"When you are inspired by some great purpose, some extraordinary project, all of your thoughts break their bonds: your mind transcends limitations, your consciousness expands in every direction and you find yourself in a new, great and wonderful world. Dormant forces, faculties and talents become alive and you discover yourself to be a greater person than you ever dreamed yourself to be."

Robin S. Sharma

CONTENTS

INTRODUCTION

To inspire someone is one of life's greatest gifts. I remember sitting around the breakfast table listening to my wife, Nancy, talk about her dream of studying a PhD. It was something she had wanted to accomplish since a child. A few years before, she had begun this area of study at Newcastle University in the UK but after only five weeks, medical issues back home forced her hand. She put her dream on hold and left the program. Now, she wanted back in.

As we sat there, I listened to her plan, her goals, and offered encouragement. I made it clear that I was in her corner, and suggested she list the top three universities she was interested in and contact them. I began to push her to take more action. I told her she would achieve her dream.

This simple breakfast time conversation had several benefits. First, Nancy appeared less stressed. She physically straightened up. Her creative flow increased and the ideas began to move more freely. Second, *I* felt lifted out of my own foggy path. I had been struggling to make ends meet as a freelance writer. My income was negligible and no matter what I seemed to start, the barriers to success appeared to grow larger with every step.

When I sat there listening and encouraging Nancy and watching the fog clear from her path, mine opened.

It is always easier to give advice than take it. I think everyone reading this will agree with that. What happened that morning was a single step forward. I stepped out of a fog, feeling the sun on my face, and while the fog was still there, it made me realize that things weren't quite so bad after all.

You see, your inspiration *is* needed. I'm not talking globally, I mean, your inspiration is needed on the street. Your wife or husband, your family member, your friends and neighbors, all need a little inspiration. They need it now more than ever.

This inspiration does not require that you forge a path down a new avenue of life, quit work, spend thousands to become a life coach, and travel the cities of America speaking to those souls in desperate need. You do not need to be Tony Robbins to do this. Tony Robbins does a fantastic job and I take my hat off to him, but there is still a need.

I heard myself say one day, 'The world appears to be falling apart.' I asked myself, 'but will changing the world 'out-there' have any effect at all, if within, *we* are the ones falling apart?'

This was a dramatic change in my thinking. I believe the world is a simple matrix, interwoven between each and every one of us. We are all part of this world, this oneness, and because of this, our influence on those around us every day is vital. How we think and feel within ourselves, influences them and us. How we act affects everyone.

No matter how bad it seems out there, by inspiring others, we can change the world. No matter the environment, or street, town, or country you live in, we can create miraculous change there, because the world is a mirror of what is going on within us. Our community thought created what is going on out there, and because of this, we can make the world a better place. By accepting the challenge to inspire, you *will* change your world.

CHAPTER TEN

AN EXTRA-ORDINARY CHALLENGE

"You don't like the world out there, change yourself." Lester Levenson

Whenever I read that quote, I feel unstoppable. Oh, what power we have within… Then I sit back and wonder, 'How?'

There are so many books, techniques and methods that lead you to find this power and use it to change yourself. The Bible, The Release technique, The Sedona Method, The Power of Quiet, books by Dr Bruce Lipton, Neale Donald Walsch, Dr Richard Bartlett, Tony Robbins, Gregg Braden, Burt Goldman and a host of others. So why am I writing this?

This is All About You

The world is a mess. I don't think I exaggerate by saying that. If you look at this from a global perspective, it's clear many are watching the world fall apart hoping someone else will fix it. We're not helping even when we want to. But what if the world out there *is* just a reflection of what's going on within us, as the above quote suggests?

If Joes on the street decided, without reservation, to make a difference, do you think the world would change? I think it would.

We've all seen or heard of people inspired to greatness by an extra-ordinary challenge. We place these people on pedestals as if they were born with neither distraction, discomfort, nor fear to derail their great project. People such as Gandhi, Mother Teresa, Buddha. But these were ordinary people who achieved extraordinary levels, because they did something most people rarely do. They placed their own interests aside and looked upon everyone as 'one' and the same.

Most never reach these lofty levels of greatness. We try to change our lives by reading books, doing courses, and workshops, or setting up New Year's resolutions. We start so determined and enthusiastic, but by week two, enthusiasm has dimmed and reality, it seems, has struck. We have not transformed into one of the X-Men or materialized a million bucks. That's not to say it can't happen, but most people don't have the patience, or the commitment required to create these things. We live in a fast food culture you see. We want everything now. If it's not dished up within seconds, we move on to the next great opportunity.

Because of this, I'm challenging you to walk a different path.

How Do You Inspire?

Every single person alive has the ability to make someone else feel great. Sometimes all it takes is a compliment to lift a person up for the entire day. Other times you must get someone to think from a new perspective no matter what has happened by asking a question such as, *"Do you see any positives to this situation?"* By focusing on inspiring others, we put our own interests aside, and in the process, we *do* inspire ourselves.

Looking at the above example of giving someone a genuine heartfelt compliment, don't you feel yourself being lifted by their reaction. There is a connection going on, on a deeper level than we are usually aware. *"You look wonderful today, your eyes are sparkling."* Your heart warms and becomes lighter when you feel *them* change within. By doing this, we bypass the

> *"MAKE OTHERS FEEL THEY CAN BECOME GREAT."* SIR RICHARD BRANSON

continual need for outside inspiration and *we* begin to change within ourselves.

With an extraordinary challenge or project in mind, we can elevate a person to a new level, or even to greatness purely by encouraging them and making them feel different about themselves within.

Even the tiniest spark can ignite a forest of dreams.

A spark has tremendous power, influence and impact.

We *are* that spark.

Unfortunately, we have forgotten how amazing we are.

MAKE YOUR LIFE AN EXAMPLE!

Live by those words.

Underneath how we imagine ourselves to be, (our body, personality, our hates, fears, wants), is a stunning energetic inspirational being radiating happiness, abundance and love.

Can you feel it?

Not yet?

Well, you will, because we *are* this incredible spark, right now, buried beneath this tangled layer of fear we've accepted as who we are over the years.

By holding on to this overburden of fear, we shield ourselves from happiness and continue down the path of fear.

The goal of this book is to embrace oneness. All for one and one for all. By looking at all of life as a web woven together by us and supported by each other, you will see that inspiring others *is* lifting ourselves.

It's time to act fearlessly and honorably and live as an example of this oneness.

My hope is this message will spread like an inspirational tsunami, one soul at a time.

IT ONLY TAKES THE TINIEST SPARK TO INSPIRE

My cousin Karen is a surgeon in a hospital in the UK. In 1985, she was a teenage punk. She dressed the part, listened to the music, and had the attitude to boot. It must have been a concern for her mom, but for her cousins, (I'm two years younger than Karen), she was just wild and cool.

My aunt visited one summer and brought her brood. Karen was dressed in black, with black make-up and ripped tights.

I'm sure my Dad had reservations, but he also knew she was smart, so one morning after breakfast he asked Karen if she had ever used a microscope? My Dad was a Pharmacologist before retiring and had a large microscope set up in his study. He placed a drop of pond water on a slide and put it under the microscope light, adjusted the settings and gave her basic instructions. That was the last we saw of Karen the entire visit. She was hooked.

I can't say this spark was transferred from my Dad to Karen, but his knowledge and understanding of the sciences certainly added to the process.

She changed almost to the second she sat down and looked through the lens of that microscope. Off came the make-up, the punk hair and clothes, the punk boyfriend, even the attitude to an extent. My Dad became a distant mentor of sorts. If she had questions, she called.

Maybe this transformation was ready to happen anyway, but the point is, with just a tiny amount of interest, Karen was offered a potential doorway to a different future.

All my Dad did was express his interest in microscopy. It just so happened this was a doorway suited for Karen.

I believe we all have them. Sometimes *we* need to open that door for others to realize the opportunity or to remember it's even there. A few years ago, my wife Nancy related a story to me about something that happened at work. (Names have been changed for privacy.)

"When I was working at the Life Enrichment Center, each month my boss would highlight an 'aha' moment, or an 'inspiring' moment to the board. I was chosen one month because of the work I did with Amanda. All I did was have her work with me in the kitchen and I helped her read the recipes. Her parents

said she had been inspired to try reading and writing again at home. She copied recipes into a journal which she gave to me as a going away present."

There was no want or need of anything in return in this example, it was simply about helping another person. What Nancy got back when she left, was to have her heart touched by someone whom she cared about. She remembered how it made her feel 'within' years later.

The payback can be simple and extra-ordinary.

ACTION - NO ACTION

Let's take the concept of inspiring others further. My Dad is an example here. He has no life coaching experience, but he inspired my cousin merely by talking to her and giving her an option: Look in the microscope lens, or don't look. She was presented with an opportunity and she took it.

Every year, at least some people who watch American Ninja Warrior, say to themselves, *I'm going to do that, I'm going to be a ninja warrior in one year.* The majority of those then reach for the Doritos and melt back into the sofa. They leave that goal as a thought, a level of no action.

We've all done it. We have a great idea, sometimes a billion-dollar idea, but we leave it at that.

Without action, it stays as a thought. It has no power as a thought.

Being Big

Most people do not take action for one reason or another. Usually it's fear. They fear they're going to fail. They fear they'll be a success. They fear they have no reason or right to put *their* idea out there. They reason that someone has already done it or can do it better. They reason a guru has said or done it, so what's the point?

We think our lives are insignificant unless we've done something big, but this isn't true. Society has deemed success as a level of material wealth and we have accepted this. It's a lie.

Most of us look at the big names, like Tony Robbins, and say, there is no way in hell I could do that. He can do it because he's Tony Robbins, but Tony Robbins has taken years to achieve the level he's at. He has not been an overnight success as many of us think. He grew up very poor in an abusive and broken home. When asked on abc-news.go.com about his biggest failure, he replied, "*I failed at a million things. I failed to achieve my goals a million times but I don't look at it as failure and that's not being positive. I look at everything as an experience to be learned from. Look at success as a result of good judgment, and good judgment is the result of experience and experience is often the result of bad judgment.*"

He has had the same fears, the same doubts about himself as anyone else, and the same level of experience or in-experience as anyone of us. He's created his persona, his charisma, his experience by presenting himself to small audiences, then larger ones, then larger ones, perfecting his craft and message. He does a hell of a job doing what he does, but Mr. Robbins can't do it all on his own. There is still a need to inspire. Your inspiration *is* still needed.

By excusing ourselves from the equation because of doubt and fear, we allow our fears to control us. It's a fear-based excuse. We excuse ourselves from taking action every day.

> *"MAKE YOUR LIFE A MASTERPIECE."*
> TONY ROBBINS

YOU *ARE* SIGNIFICANT.

You *can* influence and inspire. You *can* do what Tony Robbins does, one on one, because there is always a need to inspire.

The average person has a lot to offer. You may not be presenting to an audience of 5000, but if you can sit down in a coffee shop with a friend, or work colleague, or family member, or even a stranger, and encourage them in a goal, you can make a difference.

You may even know what a friend's goal is. They might have mentioned it again and again but have never taken action. What they need is a change in their thinking. They need to be held accountable in their actions. They need a guide.

I'm here to tell you, this is something you can do.

I'll have to prove that to you because most of us conform without realizing it.

You think you can't inspire others? You're wrong.

You do not have to be a sensation to be inspiring, the one everyone wants to be around. The one everyone wants to be friends with. The one with the amazing life experiences.

It's not that way at all.

Everyone, no matter your background, or where you grew up, no matter your level of success, financial, relational, emotional, or spiritual, we are all in this together. Each of us is affected by everyone else. By standing and stating, 'you can't,' you are effectively giving up on the future, because if one individual, one group, or nation fails to change the world, it doesn't just affect them, it affects us all.

We are all in this together. We are all capable of inspiring another. You have as much to gain or to lose as anyone else.

We convince ourselves we don't have time, or the talent, or the experience to do something. This is your limited thinking taking hold. This is your mind telling you, *'I'm not good enough,' 'I don't have the right personality,' 'I'm not inspiring,'* and the list goes on.

UNMEASURABLE POWER

These are just thoughts, nothing more, they're just thoughts. They're only powerful if you accept them and hold on to them.

These thoughts come from many influences. Family, friends, teachers, enemies, television shows, movies, books, adverts, emails, your own fears and a host of others, but it doesn't matter from where.

What matters is you realize within you lies unmeasurable power. It may not feel like it, but it's true. I will show you it's true within these pages.

Neale Donald Walsch in 'Conversations with God' said, *"you can live a charmed life by causing others to live a charmed life."* He's right.

You *can* achieve your passions and desires by helping someone else achieve theirs.

EVEN SMALL GOALS CAN BE LIFE CHANGING

Even a small amount of encouragement can change how someone else views the world. The effect can be dramatic.

My cousin's life went from punk rocker to med student and eventually to surgeon because of a look through a microscope lens at a drop of pond water.

That's an example of how simple this can be, but let's look at another example of a fear many people have.

I always had a tremendous fear of public speaking. While at university studying my Bachelors, we were often asked to present findings on a given topic to the rest of the class. Even though I knew every one of these people intimately, I was terrified. I would lose sleep the night before. I would get deathly quiet trying to shut everything out so I could focus, but I would forget things. My solution to all this was to visit the bar before class and have a few drinks to calm my nerves. As long as I still had a buzz when my time came to present, I was alright.

I'm sure you can see, this was not a cunning plan I could use to control my fear. It worked for me at the time, but I knew it was a method I couldn't continue in business or life.

Years later when writing my book '*Rockstar Lawyer*', I was asked by my co-author Greg McIntyre if I would co-present the book with him at live seminars. I said, '*Yes, of course.*' In that moment a knot of fear developed within my gut. I may have said 'yes' to Greg, but in my mind, I was immediately looking for excuses to get out of it.

I mentioned this new aspect of business to my wife who suggested I join a speaking club to learn how to speak and to gain more confidence.

To become a better public speaker, you must stand up and speak. That's essential. Her encouragement pushed me to visit a local Toastmaster's club. I joined and since then I pushed myself to give weekly impromptu and prepared speeches. I also took a position in the club where I introduced the meeting each week and tried my best to inspire and invigorate my audience. I turned my fear into a passion.

If you have a fear, you know without that first small step, the big goal will seem almost impossible.

This was one small step on a big journey, but it will send a bolt of fear through many.

Your encouragement can lift a person and help hold them up when they do not have the courage themselves, just as my wife did by suggesting the speaking club. She showed me the reasons why I needed to join.

Making yourself available to someone one-on-one, or at least to talk to them on the phone, you can encourage a new level of belief to soak in for them. By taking a little of your time to inspire a person to be better than they were, you become lifted. That will be your payment.

How You Get Paid...

My goal when I wrote *Your Inspiration is Needed* was to inspire. I was not thinking of the monetary gains I or people reading this might achieve. Although life coaching is a true profession and can be lucrative, the payment I'm referring to here is what I call 'internal payment.' This is where your sense of accomplishment and goodwill comes from filling your emotional bank.

This is the goal; energize and inspire another with no want of anything in return.

By changing your thoughts from *"how can I help myself?"* to, '*who can* I *inspire today?*' you inspire yourself. The benefits to this are unlimited and infinite and will grow the more you do it. Can you see how powerful this can be?

If you look out at the world in this moment, it should be clear that your inspiration *is* desperately needed.

You Do Not Need To Be An Expert

There are a lot of people out there wandering about dazed, trying to wave away the fog that smothers where they're headed or where they want to go. Many have no idea what they want from life. If the average person on the street was asked that question, *"what do you want to achieve in your life?*" very few could answer without stumbling over their words, or referring to lots of money, a big house and fancy car.

My focus is to help lift this fog and indecision, so the everyday person can see their life's path. This does take commitment. You must want to make a difference. This is for those who want to make a difference in the world but maybe feel they have little or nothing to offer.

What you must know is, You *can* make a difference.

Your power (as you will learn) comes from within you. Not from the world.

If you are alive, (which you are), You *can* make a difference.

If you have an intention or desire to help others and yourself, You *can* make a difference.

All it takes is to sit down with someone, listen compassionately to their message, talk with them, get them to open up, encourage and finally, hold them accountable.

You Have A Superpower

My childhood superhero was not the typical Marvel Comics superhero's, Batman, Spiderman, or Superman, it was Obi Wan Kenobi played by Alec Guinness from the original Star Wars movie.

Whether the concept of the '*force*' really sunk in, (I was only nine after all), or it was my regard for

Mr. Guinness, (my all-time favorite actor) I don't know, but something about an all-encompassing energy making up everything, flowing through us, guiding us, directing us, and empowering us, depending on our feelings of love or fear, captured me and has never left.

Try not to think me mad but I believe '*the force*' is real. We might call it something else, Morphic Fields, Universal Energy, Consciousness, or Divine Love, God, but it's the same thing underneath, it's oneness. We all have access to this incredible energy because we are this incredible energy.

Because of this, everyone has the potential to be inspired. And everyone has the potential to inspire and lift another out of the mud and move them, on an emotional level so they take action.

Do you know what that means?

It means, all of us, every one of us have a superpower. We really do.

Inspiring another *is* a superpower.

By inspiring one person, we inspire ourselves because we are all in this together. This is 'The Force' we're talking about, and we are all a part of it. Even talking to and encouraging one person has the potential to change the world.

We are limitless. We can make a difference in every aspect of our lives and in the world. Whether a change in industry, politics, religion, personal growth, all is achievable. One way to do that is to inspire others to greatness.

By doing this, we become the makers of change.

That *is* a superpower.

"RELISH THE CHALLENGE OF OVERCOMING DIFFICULTIES THAT WOULD CRUSH ORDINARY MEN AND WOMEN.'
MARK TWIGHT

SUMMARY

This *is* an extra-ordinary challenge. It is a challenge not because it is difficult to do, but because we are used to *not* doing it.

Do you feel you are a positive example to others? Many would stay silent or shake their heads when thinking of how to answer that question. Most people have a low self-impression of their positive influence on others. The reason is, so much of what we think the world is, isn't.

You have been systematically duped over your life time.

You have been programmed from birth to believe you have limited power, or no power at all. Research is now showing us something very different. It's showing us that everyone has immeasurable and unlimited power within them.

It may be tough to believe with everything going on in your life, but this power has always been there. It's been lying dormant, waiting to be ignited. This internal power proves we are significant, and truly capable of inspiring others. This is what you were born for. You are capable of amazing things already. Why should you being the example you've always hoped to be, seem like a stretch?

In the following chapter, '*We're All in this Together*', we will explore why the idea of being one with everything has been taught for thousands of years, but ignored and ignored again, and why we are still fighting tooth and nail to avoid it.

My First Challenge to You.

I challenge you to look at things from a different perspective.

This is a challenge that tests even the most determined, but it has such tremendous potential that I feel everyone should adopt it at least once.

Try at first to see a situation the way someone else sees it. For example, if you have a son or daughter and they are acting up, challenge yourself to accept their perspective, see the world through their eyes, even for a short while.

Look to understand the 'Why' of the situation.

Why *are* they doing this?

Why is *this* so important to them?

It may not resolve whatever is going on, but you can be sure *you* will have changed because of it.

A warning to you. Once you do this, you will start to think this way all the time. It will be too late to back out.

Try this a few times at home, before you take it on the road, so to speak. Your work place is an obvious location to start and can have incredible rewards for you by doing so. Again, as with a child or family member, try not to react the way you normally would. Look for the 'Why' of the situation.

It's amazing sometimes when doing this as you may have a sudden insight and want to hug the person because you finally understand their point of view. If you feel so inclined to hug them, at least ask their permission first. Let's face it, everyone could do with a hug now and then, but you still may not agree or even like their perspective. That's okay, you don't have to. It's an experiment in seeing.

CHAPTER NINE

WE'RE ALL IN THIS TOGETHER

One-ness

NOUN

1. the fact or state of being unified or whole,
   though comprised of two or more parts:
   "the oneness of man and nature"

   - identity or harmony with someone or
     something: "a strong sense of oneness is
     felt with all things"

(Definition from The Oxford Dictionary)

WHY IS ONENESS SUCH A HARD CONCEPT TO IMAGINE?

In his book *The Storm Before the Calm*, Neale Donald Walsch, who wrote the '*Conversations with God*' series said, "*How is it possible for 7 billion members of a single species to all want the same thing—survival, safety, security, peace, prosperity, opportunity, happiness, and love — and be singularly unable to produce it,*" even after all these thousands of years of trying?

How do *you* feel about that?

That's a sad statistic, right? We have heralded ourselves as such an intelligent species over the years with advancements in industry, technology, science, medicine, and yes, even weaponry, but we have failed almost completely to answer that question, '*why can't we get along?*'

For centuries, life changing messages have been spoken of, and passed down in written text by enlightened ones, past masters, and seekers of truth. We, as a society have been handed these magnificent valuable lessons, so we could free ourselves. They have not been stored away in secret for only 'the worthy' to take advantage of, they have been made available to everyone, but we have ignored them, buried them, and swept them away.

We have also been brutal with our condemnation of people who speak of a truth within us or through us, labelling those who suggest such simplicity, or claim such things as fools, dreamers, crazies and even traitors. The answer to five question *'why can't we get along'* has been handed to us again and again, but for some reason we have failed to see it, and when we have seen it, we have failed to use it.

HUMANS ARE NATURALLY NEGATIVE

You hear all the time on the air waves that, 'humans are naturally destructive, it's in our nature to destroy ourselves,' but is this really true? or have we become so accustomed to fear, hate, war, and violence that we believe it?

Are we here only to claim our piece of the prize? That little bit of land, that chunk of money, the person with the biggest stick wins mentality, or are we missing the big picture entirely?

When I looked at that question put forward by Neale Donald Walsch, I felt there was one obvious reason why after so long, we still didn't get it: Separation.

THE WAR WITHIN OURSELVES

Have you ever seen how a baby or small child reacts when taken away from its mom?

When my son was ten months old, my wife was required to go to a conference for five days.

After she kissed and hugged him, I held him up so he could wave goodbye as she drove off.

For the next day and half, I did my best to play with him, watch some shows he usually liked, fed him, kept him clean and warm, and tried to make him happy, but he cried. He would walk to the door and cry, with only the occasional laugh when tickled. He missed her from the moment she left.

He barely slept that first day, or that night, and it was only on the second day when he finally drifted off. I was exhausted when she returned, but when she walked in the living room and I saw this unconditional love and joy on his face, my energy soared.

This is how I see us.

We have separated ourselves from our true self, like a child from its mother. We deny our connection with our oneness, that thing we truly are, the all, and we hate ourselves for doing it. We are this crying child missing that connection. Not only have we separated ourselves from what we are, we've further separated ourselves in to small factions. We immediately put ourselves into these small factions by searching for others with similar ideals and beliefs.

Many groups claim undying love for all mankind on paper but curse, spit on, attack and kill any who do not agree with them. We put ourselves into these groups for protection from other groups, who do the same. We become angry if someone has a different opinion, belief, or idea. We become scared and judgmental if someone looks at things from a different perspective, who acts differently from mainstream thinking, but at the same time we claim individuality.

We are all fighting for our lives but we're fighting against ourselves, continuously, in a world and universe that *is* us. It's a war within ourselves.

AVOIDANCE OF CONFLICT

I have been releasing for years, on and off. Releasing is a way of ridding ourselves of the negative feelings we have collected over our lives. I have also been avoiding. I have avoided conflict. I have avoided arguments. I have avoided giving my opinion in case it offended others. I have avoided life by nearly always staying clear of being judged, or having approval taken away from me.

This was something I only recently accepted about myself. I have been afraid of this for too long. I questioned how I should change. Should I start to jump in to conflict, speak my mind with no care if I offend others? Should I speak purely to illicit an opposing response?

As I thought about this, I wondered how many people do exactly the same thing? Do we go out of our way to remain silent on those issues that could cause the greatest conflict because we want others to like us, or we don't want them to dislike us? Do we hold our tongues to get approval?

We will often criticize those who speak their minds, especially if it goes against general mainstream thinking of the day. We often stay silent even though we may agree with what's been said so as not to lose approval.

I am, of course, generalizing, or at least I think I am.

Aren't most people after approval from whoever they meet? Don't most people want to be liked, rather than being disliked? So, maybe I'm not generalizing.

Should we all stand and deliver a message no matter what the repercussions?

Now, hold on a minute…

Conflict for conflicts sake doesn't work. It never has. So, should we speak up, or not speak up? Make up your mind.

1) Avoidance does not help. You are basically ignoring an issue hoping it will go away, suppressing your feelings for the good of who? The Suppression of your feelings is probably the worst thing to do. Trust me, I know.

2) So then, speak your mind, give an opinion, even if you know it will cause conflict. But creating conflict, or adding to conflict, will not solve anything.

3) We think of our opinions as aggressively pursuing an objective but giving an opinion can bring about discussion and solution. It doesn't have to be aggressive. An opinion does not necessarily mean disagreement and conflict. By energizing a discussion with your opinion, we move potential issues forward. By avoiding issues, or being scared of losing approval, we kill off potential.

We should embrace the possibility and potential of change.

I have been scared for too long. Do you feel the same?

I want people to get interested in a discussion. I want you to feel a need to amplify opinion, not provoke, but to create new thinking in old ideas and subjects.

WE'RE ALL IN THIS TOGETHER AFTER ALL

The world is suffering from stage four terminal cancer because we're convinced we can't get along with ourselves. [1] The only way to cure this cancer

---

[1] And no, it is not about irradiating ourselves with nuclear war to cure the cancer, that is the old outdated Newtonian cure.

is to change our thinking about it by looking at the world and everything on it as part of this oneness. We must stop separating ourselves.

Whether you believe in Christianity, Judaism, Islam, Hinduism, Buddhism, Confucianism, or if you are an atheist, does not matter. 'Oneness' is what feels right to you. It is about being in harmony with all of humanity, not about religion. Through the ages we have identified this idea of universal consciousness as many things. You can call it God, life, universal spirit, universal consciousness, subconsciousness, qi, or holy spirit, it doesn't matter.

THE MAP

I have often looked at the concept of beliefs as a map. Take the United States as an example. For arguments sake, let's say everyone starts off their life journey in New York City. Our goal in this life is to make it across the map to San Francisco.

(In my opinion, the purpose of life is the same for everyone, to find happiness and love, no matter which path you take.)

San Francisco in this example, is happiness and love. So, we all start out from New York City on our journey. Some take the direct, fastest route, directly through the center states. Others take a more scenic route north through South Dakota, and others go south to visit the Grand Canyon on the way. Still others start on one route and change, then change again, depending on their life circumstances, but we all eventually make it to San Francisco. Why is one route deemed better than the others? It just comes down to what feels right to you at the time.

There have been many realized masters over the years. [2] One of them was a physicist called Lester Levenson. He changed his thinking from *wanting* to be loved, to one of *being* loving. In so doing, he became freer and lighter in the burdens his body carried, and happier.

Like many masters, he didn't stop at his own realization but wanted to share this wonderous discovery with what he called, *"the rest of me."*

'The rest of me', refers to 'oneness', a realization that everything, all people, all animals, all plants, all alien species throughout the universe, are part of one thing. We're all in this together. We're all a part of this oneness.

When we grasp this concept of oneness and accept it, and we will eventually, the world out there will change over-night.

---

[2]   The word 'Master' has many definitions but from my perspective, a Master is someone who has lifted the veil and seen what life is really all about. A Master is not someone who has read about it and understood the concept merely on a conscious level but has actually experienced a change in their very being.

An Example of Oneness

Gandhi was an ordinary man until he realized power was not something out there in the world, it is an inner manifestation. You become externally what you are within. Gandhi knew this. He looked at the world as one thing. His leadership defeated the largest, most influential empire the world had ever seen without throwing a punch. He beat the British Empire within himself by accepting the empire's actions as an issue within himself. Gandhi showed how the impossible becomes possible when you hold only love in your heart.

> *"THE DIFFERENCE BETWEEN WHAT WE ARE DOING AND WHAT WE ARE CAPABLE OF DOING WOULD SOLVE MOST OF THE WORLD'S PROBLEMS."* ~ Mahatma Gandhi

Through an acceptance of oneness, it is easier to let go of the issues of the world. What is happening out there is merely a reflection of what is happening within. Let go of the issues within and the world out there changes.

Think what you can do if you focus your attention, not on your fears, hates, frustrations, wants or desires out-there, but instead, on ridding your world 'within' of these things. I recommend you journal your progress. Using a daily journal can naturally bring in to your awareness, issues you are holding on to. It can help you find your path. (See chapter six for an example of a Gain Journal entry and the appendix for a list of resources.)

Do You Realize You're Not Even Close to Your True Potential?

The reason I included a chapter on 'oneness' is because of how society currently evaluates life. Our time in this world has been diminished over the years to a set of rules. Dare I say it, but we have been turned in to batteries for the economy and power of nations.

There is a happiness index which rates each country as to how happy their citizens are, but the parameters are sketchy at best. *"The researchers straight-up asked people to rank their own happiness. These answers are then weighted based on six other factors: levels of GDP, life expectancy, generosity, social support, freedom and corruption."* [3]

While this can be looked at as a positive step, it also focuses the attention on looking at the world out-there for the answers to happiness. (Each factor is based on what the world can do for me, rather than what I can do for the world.) Find a

---

[3]   https://www.sciencealert.com/
       the-world-happiness-index-2016-jus
       t-ranked-the-happiest-countries-on-earth.

country higher up the scale, move there, and you may become a happier person.

Yes, there are benefits to this, it is a positive step but the over-riding process for anyone being asked these questions is to look out at the world and gauge their happiness on what they don't want to accept in life. Look at freedom for instance. I would gauge my freedoms on a scale of 1-10, (10 being the best) as may be a 7. I do that partly because of political turmoil in my country, but also by how terrible people's freedoms are in other countries. My answer is based on how I view the world. I may have a friend living up the street who answers that same question with a 9 or a 2 also dependent on their views and psychology of the world at the time.

If you look for happiness through money, your country's freedoms, life expectancy and such, you are evaluating the individual, separate from the all. Your happiness is therefore dependent on factors which you have limited or no control over.

If you turn this on its head and focus on your family, friends, neighbors, and yes even politicians as being one with you, each being an '*individua-tion*' of oneness, your view of the world changes.

I know this is not the easiest thing to do. When I asked my friend to edit this chapter he had a real problem with the concept of oneness, especially with politicians. He wanted to know how to stop separating ourselves from someone you strongly disagree with?

THE HOLOGRAM OF ONENESS

"You are not only living in the universe, the universe is living within you."
Dr Jean Houston

Every part of a hologram right down to the smallest element, holds the entirety of the hologram within it. The idea of the universe being within us then becomes transparent when thinking holographically, because then every atom holds the entirety of the universe within it.

We have the power to change our lives, our health, our financial situations, even our DNA

"BOHN'S INTERPRETATION OF QUANTUM PHYSICS INDICATED THAT AT THE SUBQUANTUM LEVEL, THE LEVEL IN WHICH THE QUANTUM POTENTIAL OPERATED, LOCATION CEASED TO EXIST. ALL POINTS IN SPACE BECAME EQUAL TO ALL POINTS IN SPACE, AND IT WAS MEANINGLESS TO SPEAK OF ANYTHING AS BEING SEPARATE FROM ANYTHING ELSE."
MICHAEL TALBOT

---

by how we think and which thoughts we allow to take seat in our minds.

If just one person changes their perceptions from love to fear, the universe changes suit. It has no choice. You are directing the play with your thinking.

If just one person changes their perceptions from fear to love, the universe changes suit. Again, it has no choice.

We do this all the time, not only while meditating or having the intention of peace and love, but when we are angry, frustrated, hateful, judgmental, or living in fear. This change might be very subtle at first. For years we have piled negativity on top of our true loving feelings, burying them. Depending on how much garbage you have accumulated can determine whether you feel a difference at first. Eventually you *will* feel a change by removing the garbage. Inspiring others is just one way to do that.

Oneness with the universe is within us, always.

A Simple Experiment

On the previous page, I mentioned a friend who asked how to stop separating ourselves from someone we strongly disagree with. So, imagine for a minute you are part of only one thing. Everyone out there, no matter who, including yourself, is part of this one thing, no longer separated by distance, space, height, weight, color, beliefs, time or anything, we are just one.

Think for example, what would happen if your blood was racing around your body and each blood vessel thought of itself as separate and individual from all the others. I know it's not easy to do but give it a try.

Write down your feelings and thoughts about this.

Now imagine the issues you see in others, (how you dislike so and so because they're messy, or have had it too easy, or have an annoying voice, or are too damn loud and opinionated, whatever it is).

"WE ARE ALL ONE. ALL THINGS ARE ONE THING. THERE IS ONLY ONE THING, AND ALL THINGS ARE PART OF THE ONE THING THERE IS. THIS MEANS THAT YOU ARE DIVINE. YOU ARE NOT YOUR BODY, YOU ARE NOT YOUR MIND, AND YOU ARE NOT YOUR SOUL. YOU ARE THE UNIQUE COMBINATION OF ALL THREE, WHICH COMPRISES THE TOTALITY OF YOU. YOU ARE AN INDIVIDUATION OF DIVINITY; AN EXPRESSION OF GOD ON EARTH."
NEALE DONALD WALSCH.

Imagine them as just emotions you are holding within you.

Next, try to accept (even momentarily) that these emotions are just fears, hates, frustrations, and desires within you. The only reason you see them in other people is because those things exist in you. (Remember, being one with everything, we share the responsibilities.)

You may have to dig deep to see these things in yourself as you have so many barriers, ego-based controls and self-belief programs as to who you are. It may not be necessary to uncover those feelings but try to get a glimpse of them nonetheless.

I know some of you might be offended by the idea that what you see as negative in someone else, is in fact a negative within yourself. It can be hard to accept this, especially when the frustration or anger is at its height. '*My neighbor, or boss, or that politician, is a loud, unpleasant jerk and I am not like that!*'

A friend of mine, Adam, like many, was frustrated and even revolted with the idea of being compared to politicians of our day. He wrote to me about the concept of being 'One' with everyone and voiced his frustrations. '*I have read the chapter you sent and I think it's good, quite inspirational and I can relate to some of what you're saying. I must be honest though, as soon as you mentioned having oneness with politicians I found it hard to relate to. Like a lot of people in the UK I feel strongly about the fact that we're committing financial suicide by leaving the EU, not to mention loss of workers' rights, lack of EU workers in jobs where we really need them, divisiveness and all the other things that may happen, because certain politicians had a referendum in the first place which completely divided the country.*

Then, to top it all, they fed false facts to people. Then there is the destruction of the NHS and loads more! I also could never imagine having oneness with someone as divisive as Trump. Also have you read the papers lately? Sorry, I think I've become a bit disillusioned with things."

These are real feelings and I understand why people have them, I really do. I have experienced the same feelings when I think of certain people or specific events. My stomach develops a knot, or I'm instantly on edge and a wave of anger floods upwards. But once I step away from these emotions and begin to look at things through a different set of shades, call them your 'Power Shades,' the anger, frustrations, that whole sea of negativity can leave. Doing this is an incredible eye opener. It can change so much for you, if you give it a chance. Also remember that it is you, (not the person you are angry with,) that is carrying these negative feelings around. It's not hurting whoever you're angry/ frustrated with at all, it only hurts you and those closest to you.

By trying to overcome this revulsion, just for a minute, and search for that loving nature within you, a door to a whole new perception of the world can open for you. Each of us see the world not the way it is, but as a reflection of ourselves.

By accepting issues that you see in others as reflections of your inner self, you can bring these issues buried deep within you to the surface, making them conscious. Only when they are conscious can you free yourself from them.

Most of us don't know the emotional barriers we hold within ourselves, and if you don't know they're there, how can you deal with them?

I'm saying this, so you can realize your potential.

Now, whatever you see in others, think of it merely as a guide asking you to free it. Say to it, 'you are free to leave.'

Keep doing this until you no longer feel this negativity towards whoever it is.

It is a great system if we listen and use it.

If we listen, we can realize how together we really are. Oneness is not such a stretch after all. If we don't listen, life will stay as it is, or become a self-created hell.

Let me ask you one more thing about this subject.

How does it feel to you when you see a politician, for example, acting or saying things that you think are stupid, ridiculous, crazy or whatever?

Is it a good feeling?

Does it make your life and the lives of those around you better for having this feeling?

By trying this, and looking at it merely as an interesting experience, you can allow yourself to be far happier than you were. Isn't that reason enough to try it. After all, how does you getting upset and lowering your power going to bother the person you are angry or frustrated at? It won't. It will not make the slightest bit of difference to them. In fact, it is a business tactic, well known and utilized to self-promote. Get haters to advertise your message, because they will scream so much louder than those who support you. (G.McIntyre / R.Christiansen. 2017 Rockstar Lawyer.)

MAGIC BY EMERGENCE

I have asked myself, 'what is inspiration?' So far, I have focused my attention on inspiring someone to move forward with a goal, whether in business or personal life. This ranges from helping them ease out the stuckness swamp when starting in a new area of business, finding clarity, or encouraging them to take that first step and join a gym.

All these are relevant, but inspiration can touch any area of life. It is limitless in its application, and if used in certain ways, a much more impactful transformation can occur. Dr Bruce Lipton when talking about initiating global evolution, said, "*There is a process called emergence which says, when you bring enough parts together, what happens to those parts is greater than anybody could imagine by looking at any of the individual parts alone. In other words, something new comes out of the community that you could never anticipate by looking at any of the individuals in the community. This is what we are looking forward to, a state of emergence, a state of new belief, a state of consciousness, and this will be the most amazing because the collective power of seven billion humans working together in harmony will generate a world that at this moment we couldn't even envision, and it's right at our doorstep."*

Think of the impact a little inspiration can have? 'Your inspiration is needed' can be about inspiring love in another person, inspiring compassion in another, inspiring happiness or oneness in another, inspiring peace and quiet of mind in another. The compounding inspiration can take on a life of its own.

How you inspire others is open to what is most important to you. By needing your inspiration, we are needing that which is most inspiring to you, that thing that bubbles up within you, where you can hardly hold yourself back in all the passion and excitement that flows out. This can manifest in others. All these things and more are needed.

EVERYONE IS AN INSPIRATION

All of us, no matter where we are in life, are inspirational beings. Most of us are not as well-known as those who have touched the hearts of millions, but we are no less capable.

Think of it this way, each of us is assisting in bringing about a more connected world. Whether we assist just one or one million, we are still as loving, compassionate and inspirational. It's not the number of people we help but *that* we help. Helping just one, has the potential to inspire the entire planet. You don't know how influential you could be? I'm sure people such as Jesus and Martin Luther King Jr did not realize how deep and how long their influence would penetrate in to society.

That one person you inspire to move, to reach for the stars, may create a new path, product or service which improves the lives of millions, or saves the oceans from pollution, or helps us look past our differences. Yes, these are 'out-there' in the world solutions, but as stated earlier, if a solution moves us to change within, then it has the potential to create major change on the outside.

If you are reading this book, it shows you have been looking at the world, the universe, and yourself from a different perspective. You understand there is more than what we've been told. You might not know what it is, but you know there is something most people miss.

> "THE MORE AND MORE EACH IS IMPELLED BY THAT WHICH IS INTUITIVE, OR THE RELYING UPON THE SOUL FORCE WITHIN, THE GREATER, THE FARTHER, THE DEEPER, THE BROADER, THE MORE CONSTRUCTIVE MAY BE THE RESULT." - EDGAR CAYCE 792-2

Inspiration is not something only a few possess. We are born inspired and have that always. It is the programs we've accepted in our lives, mostly as children, that cloud and cover our true potential. For example, *'money does not grow on trees'*. By accepting such programming when young, we unconsciously build on them and defend them throughout our lives until the programs stand as truth behind walled castles in our minds. But they are just our past thinking we are holding on to. The inspired loving 'you' is still there, it's just covered up by the garbage.

"Even when the sky is heavily overcast, the sun hasn't disappeared. It's still there on the other side of the clouds."
Eckhart Tolle

In our most dire moments, those times when life feels like it is crashing down on us and the only thoughts we have are those of our impending doom, it is at those moments when you can hear your guiding angels telling you, *'this is your moment, this is the time you can release your chains and swim straight to the surface'*. All you have to do is thank yourself, or God, or the universe, or the great spirit, for showing you what you are holding on to, so you have the opportunity to free it. Then it's gone. The burden you carried for so long has been dropped.

I know I am making out that this process is simple. I know how it is when everything feels like it's against you, and fear envelops you. You fear your health is failing, your prospects are non-existent, your looks are going, your skin is sagging, your hair is graying, you're getting out of shape, you hate your job, boss, house, car, but have no money to fix them. So much lack comes to mind. Fear after fear, never ending. But do you realize the opportunity laid out right there?

I state in chapter 8 that we have been '*served up a smorgasbord of the finest of everything, yet we ignore it and instead pick at the scraps in the trash, complaining the whole time how unfair it is.*' Even though we have been told this over and over, century after century, we still cry and pick from the scraps in the trash. If you don't know what you are holding on to, (those programs you have accepted over the years), how can you get rid of them? **This *is* your opportunity**!

Each of us place our mark on the world whether we know it or not.

Our imprint is embedded in the very fabric of the world every second of every minute of every day. How we feel is how the world functions. The more lightened you feel within from the act of lifting others to new heights of inspiration, will have a reciprocating effect on the world. We are a part of the oneness, and so the input of each person on the planet is as vital and telling as anyone else.

We are all in this together. That is what we have.

SUMMARY

- o There is a connection throughout the universe that bonds us all. We are all in this together. There is no alternative, and it's about time we did something about it.

How much longer can we ignore our own pain and unhappiness?

Oneness is not about living lives of lack and normalcy. It's about being extra-ordinary. You can't help being extra-ordinary because underneath all the accumulated baggage you have collected over your life, you are an amazing, loving being, that knows and feels a connection to everything. Oneness is about showing that.

Everyone's life affects everyone else's life, but we are generally unaware how influential we really are. The movie 'It's a Wonderful Life,' was a perfect example of how most, if not all people's lives affect the lives of others without ever knowing it.

We are rarely given the insight George Bailey was gifted by seeing what life would be like if we had never been born. Yes, it's Hollywood, but even so, if you or I were asked how, or if we made life better for those in our lives, most would fail to see our true impact.

The reality is, we all make an impression on others, for good, and sometimes not so good. With just a little more awareness and heart-based effort, we can make a supreme difference in the world.

So, you see, you really are the richest person in town. Start thinking of yourself as such.

As a part of the all, you have been gifted with a great opportunity to make a difference. In the following chapter 'An Opportunity Every Second', we will address some of the soul sucking scenarios the world has accepted as truth, and how to turn them on their heads.

MY SECOND CHALLENGE TO YOU.

You knew this was coming. I challenge you to focus on someone who rattles you. They don't have to be your sworn enemy, or someone who makes you froth at the mouth, but it is clear you find them offensive for whatever reason. Use the steps outlined in this chapter (highlighted below) and see their negativity, their pain as your negativity, or your pain.

1- Imagine you and that person as one, no longer separated by distance, space, height, weight, color, beliefs, time or anything, we are just one. At least try to do this.

2- Now imagine the issues you see in this person, (how you dislike them because they're messy, or have had it too easy, or have an annoying voice, or are too damn loud and opinionated, whatever it is), and try to accept (even momentarily) that these are just the fears, hates, frustrations, and desires you have within *you*. The only reason you see them in other people is because those things exist in you. Try to overcome any revulsion at doing this, just for a minute.

3- Now, whatever you see in them, think of it merely as a guide asking you to free it. Say to it, *'you are free to leave.'*

4- Keep doing this until you no longer feel this negativity towards the person. Test it out the next time you see them. Whether they're on television or in person, it makes no difference.

CHAPTER EIGHT

AN OPPORTUNITY IN EVERY MOMENT

Opportunity is the word we use when something in the world occurs that offers us hope. The opportunity to make more money, the opportunity to get a great new job, the opportunity to move to that town or city, the opportunity to meet that person who is just right for us.

Whatever your hope is, there is opportunity everywhere to bring it forth. It surrounds us in every moment of life, even in places deemed to be 'hell on earth' there is the greatest opportunity for growth, but we rarely see the opportunity for what it is. Why is this?

Our world is saturated by fear, hate and insecurity. Simply turn on your television or open your computer to witness another war, another murder, rape, hate based crime, greed, control, disease, addiction, suicide, sadness and disillusionment. By looking at the world 'out there' it appears we are living on the edge of hell.

So how can a world constantly flooding in such horrors *be* an inspiring opportunity?

As with any circumstance in life, there are multiple ways to look at it.

For instance, if you look out at the world, what do you see? Do you focus on beautiful landscapes, trees with leaves changing color, the sun sparkling off lakes and rivers, and the love and care of friends and family? Or, do you focus on poverty, hurt, pain, struggle, and see no end in sight? Or are you somewhere in between?

Now ask yourself, where are those feelings coming from when you focus on these things? These feelings only come from within us.

Another way to look at this situation is to understand the true meaning of opportunity.

According to Collins English dictionary, the word 'Opportunity' can be defined as meaning:

1. a favorable, appropriate, or advantageous combination of circumstances

2. a chance or prospect

Whatever the situation that surrounds you, or the circumstances you focus on most, no matter how heartbreaking, draining, or daunting it may seem, if you can break through that negativity even for a second, you will see there is an opportunity. Hand-in-hand with any problem, comes a solution. The opportunity is the solution. It is waiting for you to open up.

One specific understanding about opportunity that emerges is, 'Opportunity' is not 'out-there' in the world at all, it is within us. The opportunity to change things for the better is found within you and me. This is why there is an opportunity in every moment.

For a long time, I believed as many do, that these horrors were the result of poor leadership, power hungry governments, greed and lack, revolving around the control of planetary resources. Control of fresh water, land for farming, control of a population through educational and health conditioning. I saw no benefit to these practices except to those in power. But by examining our world in a different light, everything and every moment, no matter what it is, becomes the potential for opportunity.

That is going to feel pretty harsh to those reading this who have experienced something they see as negative, such as the loss of a job, or an accident of some kind, and if that is the case, and you find yourself struggling with this, I urge you to give this a chance and listen to the message within these pages. It *is* that important.

Why *I* Think **O**pportunity **A**bounds.

Let me define what *I* mean by 'opportunity'.

First of all, I am not suggesting all the negatives mentioned above are wonderful, great events that must be embraced with dignity and a smile.

What I am saying is each of the issues mentioned are 'out there' in the world issues. I believe they exist because of the accumulated fear, the negative thinking and feelings that we, as a global society hold on to. Just look at how people react to a winter storm down here in North Carolina. At the first mention of snow on the news, a mad panic ensues. Hordes of people rush to the grocery stores and buy out the milk and bread departments, even though the snow in our town never lasts more than a few days. It's a display of fear, of 'what ifs'.

Society has a fascination burgeoning on obsession with fear and negativity. We are entertained by it in movies, we are horrified and frustrated by it when watching or reading the news which floods our senses every minute of every day. All this has conditioned us to look at fear as a normal part of our lives. We hold in our minds and our hearts all these negativities that have soaked in over the years.

Our collective habit of holding these things to heart, (within ourselves), results in what we see every day. *We* create these things. We create the life we see in the world.

The issue is, if what we hold in mind *is* creating the world out there, then looking for the answers 'out there' will not solve the problems, unless by solving a problem 'out there' creates a change within us.

One Solution

I say this is just one solution because there are *many* different paths to reaching the goal, (see text under The Map subheading in the previous chapter).

One way to change what we see and experience in the world 'out there,' is to change what is going on within us.

"WE SEE THE WORLD, NOT AS IT IS, BUT AS WE ARE." ANONYMOUS.

This is why 'Opportunity' is *always* within us.

By changing ourselves from within, we change our own world. By inspiring others to change within speeds up this process, we change the world 'out there' together.

"I can honestly tell you as I sit here right now, if there is a heaven, I think it is absolutely right here, right now. It was always here and think about it, what is heaven? A place of creation... If I created hell in my former heaven, that's what I saw was the hell. But today I don't go there. I have much

healthier, happier thoughts and the creations follow those thoughts directly, so I'm overjoyed about life as you can see because I was the guy who didn't believe in any of this stuff." Dr Bruce Lipton.

With this in mind, I believe it is clear, we are living in a time where heaven, freedom, unconditional love, a positive framework for all life, call it what you will, is served to us on a beautiful glowing silver platter with fireworks going off either side of it. The opportunity to change the picture out there is always available to us, every single second of every moment. The opportunity is always there.

Allow me to explain further.

In chapter five I discuss the use of core values, our guiding principles in life, and show you my own top eight core values. This is my number 7 Core Value: *Everything happening in the world is a reflection of what is happening within. Use what is happening in the world to let go of your attachments to it.*

Use What Is Happening In The World As A Guide

If you look at what is happening in the world as your guiding light, a way of seeing what you are holding onto within yourself, the opportunity can become obvious.

Take for example, the fear and anger that arises when a bill comes through from the Doctor's office, or from a hospital visit. The bill is usually far higher than you ever expected. I use this example because this happened to me in 2017. Upon opening the envelop, I saw the dollar amount they were billing me, $5725. At first, I was shocked, then anger flowed up and eventually, after I stepped back and wondered what the hell to do, I started to worry. My over-riding thought was, "*I am* not *paying this. How the hell can they gouge this much. I was in the emergency room for two and half hours, that was it.*" No amount of discussion with my wife helped. She pointed out the potential discounts we could get by being uninsured, but I was determined. I felt I had been taken advantage of.

I knew what I felt was inside me. I knew having this feeling was not going to help my situation. I knew getting angry at the hospital administration was not going to help. I knew there was the chance this anger would be passed on to my family by getting angry with them for not having the same view as me.

By holding on to these feelings, I was throwing gasoline on to the fire, making the whole situation far worse.

Was it a difficult situation? Yes. I was barely making ends meet with my work at the time. But by sitting down, quietly reflecting on all that was happening, I got to the point where I could ask myself a question:

"*What is the opportunity here?*"

Sometimes you can ask this question, but the answer is clouded in a thick fog. This is because you are still holding all the negatives in your heart. You rack your mind to think of how this can be so great an opportunity, and nothing comes up. Money has a tendency to do that. No matter what you think, there's a tendency to feel you're losing out. But by simply asking the question, '*What is the opportunity here?*' you are stepping forward. It might be only one step out of the fog surrounding you, but even that is better than wallowing in self-pity and anger. Staying where you were will not resolve the situation or open you up to the opportunity. You will just spiral down into more and more negativity and begin to hate yourself for it.

When I asked this question, the heavens did not open with a check for the amount I owed. What did happen was a new perspective. The opportunity for me was to allow years of frustration at how poorly the medical fraternity is run to dissolve. I had been holding this in for years.

Whenever I went to see a doctor, I would feel disempowered and depressed. It was a feeling that no matter what I did, I felt control was being taken from me. That's not a good feeling. By asking this question, I realized that control was mine after all.

It was just a decision I had had before to hand control over to the doctor.

The other reason I have used this example is because so many people in America are experiencing this same situation, or something similar.

Every time something shows up that bothers you, an opportunity has been presented to you to set that thought free. By setting it free, it is no longer being held hostage within you.

ANGEL GUIDES

I try to look at whatever is going on in my life as my guiding angel pointing out to me, "*hey, you still haven't let go of this. I'm going to keep banging on the door until you listen and release your attachment to it.*" That's what my guiding angel says to me.

With regards to my costly visit to the emergency room for a bout with asthma one night, I did my best to allow my feelings of anger and loss of control to leave. After doing this, I sent the hospital and the bill of $5725 my love with no attachments or conditions to it. Just love and nothing less. I really felt this love in my heart.

The next day after my wife again suggested I should call to see what, if any discounts we could get on the bill, I called the number provided. After giving my account number and name, I waited. Whatever dread or thought about what was to come entered my mind, I allowed it to leave and gave it my love. Then the woman taking my call came back on the phone. She pleasantly announced to me that the bill in question had been readjusted to zero. I was shocked. For a few seconds all I could say was, 'er.' Then I thanked her as if she had personally done this just for me.

Did this result come about directly because I allowed the anger, frustration, and worry to leave, and then felt love for the very thing I was worried about? *I* believe it was, but I can't say for sure. Even if it wasn't, I had allowed these negativities to leave, regardless of the bill, and my life was happier for doing so.

My angel guide was much happier for a while, sitting quietly with just a nudge now and then, until the next big issue arose. Now, sometimes, I do tell my angel where to go, but as I now realize that this doesn't help much, (as the issue just keeps coming back), I try to look upon whatever it is from a different perspective.

Your angel does not have to be a typical angel flitting about on delicate wings and sparkling like a diamond. Mine changes now and then but more often than not I imagine the actor Alec Guinness as Obi Wan Kenobi from the original Star Wars movie as my angel guide. Call it a cliché if you want, I don't mind, because the imagery works for me. No one else is going to hear or see your angel after all.

This is a conversation with limitlessness, a conversation with God even, if you allow it to be.

EATING SCRAPS FROM THE TRASH

We have allowed the external circumstances in the world to control us. We look at the economy to improve our finances, the next president to make a difference for us, the company we work for to help make our lives better, a product to improve us, the television series we watch each week to take the frustrations away for a short while. We believe our happiness is dependent on these things, and most see no end in sight to the everyday dramas.

It's become a requirement to reach for perfection in every aspect of our lives. We want to be better, or richer, or faster, or stronger, or grander, or smarter, or more impressive, more expensive, more beautiful, more powerful, more, more, more, always more.

The crazy thing is, we *are* creating our lives, every aspect of them, our finances, the relationships we're in, our health, the type of people we constantly meet no matter where we live. The reason we don't see this is because we only look 'out there' in the world to achieve these things. We rarely, if ever, look within. Either we don't know we create it all, don't accept we create it all, or know it and accept it but it's so ingrained in us to search out there, that we're constantly sidelined and refuse to put in the necessary time to change it.

Why?

We have been served up a smorgasbord of the finest of everything, yet we ignore it and instead pick at the scraps in the trash complaining the whole time how unfair it is.

Why don't we see this magnificent feast in front of us?

Why do so many struggle with such a simple system?

SIMPLICITY EQUALS LACK OF SUBSTANCE

One thing that seems apparent is our desire to over-complicate life. If something looks too simple we tend to dismiss it as not having the substance to make significant change, but the reality is exactly the opposite.

Over complication brings in the ego mind to try and figure out the problem. The ego uses 'out there' in the world solutions, that's all it has. We cannot solve things by searching 'out there'.

Over complication is often the ego mind wanting to control and have power over others. Haven't you felt a twinge of power by making a solution a bit more clever than it needs to be?

The answers to life's problems are usually so simple many of us walk right by them.

If It's Not Here This Second!

For example, have you ever put in an order at a fast food restaurant, then stood there tapping your fingers, getting a little frustrated by how long your food was taking?

Have you ever opened your emails and become angry that it took five seconds for a new window or attachment to open?

Have you ever sat at a red light and complained that the idiot in front took two seconds too long to react to the green?

We have become conditioned to want everything now. Just a few seconds more creates anger, frustration and even violence.

I believe there are good clear reasons for this. One reason is the illusion of a separate existence.

What do I mean by that?

Separation and Oneness: The Wood for the Trees

When I write about oneness, it is a subject I have researched, thought about, written, dreamt of, and know so well on a conscious level that sometimes when I'm trying to explain it to someone, I miss the simplicity and clarity needed to be understood. It's like trying to act out 'nothingness' in charades. It sounds easy but when you stand up to do it, no one gets what you're trying to say.

Let's face it, 'Oneness' is not something we can experience with our current level of thinking, it's just too far out there. To know oneness, we must remove the mind/ego from the equation because it is the mind that convinces us we are an individual separate from the all.

Understanding oneness requires intent and to allow acceptance that it's possible without ever having any solid conscious experience of it. It's not exactly faith, because faith is a feeling within, a knowing. So, understanding and accepting oneness is theoretical, unless you have seen through the fog.

> *"Einstein revealed that we do not live in a universe with discrete, physical objects separated by dead space. The universe is one indivisible, dynamic whole in which energy and matter are so deeply entangled it is impossible to consider them as independent elements."* Dr Bruce Lipton.

I believe we are all part of this oneness. I believe there *is* no separation, but we've become convinced there is, which we hate. We hate ourselves for not feeling this oneness anymore which subconsciously we know we are. That's why I believe we fill our lives with so much excess. We try to cover up this deep-down feeling of loss by buying stuff.

Self-hatred has become so common place we rarely even recognize it. We want to place blame on something, so we disapprove of ourselves, and as we're all part of this oneness, everyone else is included in that disapproval. You express hate/anger/frustration at a server for not being fast enough, not because they are slow but because you have that negativity within you. You only see that negativity in others because it exists in you. When you find that negativity, you can release it, and the situation 'out there' will dissolve away.

By expressing unconditional love to one another, you are connecting oneness. People respond in kind because there is always a desire within us to connect back to oneness.

Do you see how simple that is?

Self-Doubt

No matter what your external out in the world situation is, if you don't deal with your internal 'within' struggles, your external world will keep showing you the same stuff.

Example: If you are miserable because you only have a little money in your bank, even if you come into millions, you will still be miserable, only you will be miserable in more comfort. Yes, you would have a temporary feeling of happiness from a lottery win, but it would be fleeting. Soon you would realize you are still not happy even with the money. If you change that lack of happiness from within, your experience with money and any other external object would change immediately.

Money, cars, houses, watches etc., only provide us ways to fill the void within us.

You feel unhappy, so you buy something cool, and POW, the happiness floods back, temporarily. Then you have a wonderful solution, buying stuff, and there you have the issue with much of society. Instead of dealing with the issue, we have an easy 'out' button. This button includes any number of addictions: Alcohol, drugs, sex, food.

We buy stuff to fill our sieve with happiness. Then we must buy more to stay happy. It's an addiction. We are essentially addicts, until we look at where the problems in life really are and change that.

Your internal problems follow you no matter where you go. You carry them with you all the time.

Whatever life hands you, it will go on and on unless you address the internal issues. They don't go away on their own.

> *"PEOPLE ARE ADDICTED TO THEIR BELIEFS."* MICHAEL TALBOT.

Changing the external world will only temporarily deal with internal issues. You leave a town for another hoping the change of scenery will change your life for the better, but you quickly find you pick up where you left off, you're just in a different environment with different names around you.

But changing your internal situation *will* change your world 'out there'. It's the only way to ever get ahead.

SUMMARY

- o Opportunity is being handed to us every single second of every single day. Much of the time we walk right by the opportunity or get caught up in the *'sky is falling'* scenarios we see every day on the news or from doomsayers.

But things are not as bleak as we have been led to believe. The answers to our most important questions are there in plain sight if we would just open our eyes.

- o Our angel guides are there for us. I'm sure by now they are beginning to scream as we continually ignore them. But they are still there. Every situation that occurs and causes you pain, is a tap on your shoulder saying, *'are you going to give this permission to leave yet?'* Whether you believe in angels or not is irrelevant. Use a more scientific analogy if it helps but use one.

In the following chapter 'The Universe Within', we will explore further one of the conundrums affecting us all. If what we hold in mind *is* creating the world out there, then looking for the answers 'out there' will not solve our problems.

We go searching and seeking answers for the world's problems 'out there' all the time, but are these answers just temporary delusions we hold to our hearts to make ourselves feel better?

MY THIRD CHALLENGE TO YOU.

I challenge you to use what is happening in the world as your guiding light, (those things that frustrate or anger you) as a way of seeing what you're holding onto within yourself. Document these things in your Gain Journal.

This is a major life lesson. If this was taught to kids in kindergarten school, the world would become a much happier place as they grew into adulthood.

So, what steps can you follow:

1- Focus on one source of negativity that pops up in your life. Something small to begin with. For example, the driver in front of you takes too long to turn left at a light.

2- Simply observe what you notice about this thing.

3- What comes up from within you?

4- Imagine your angel guide, that guiding light being available to help you whenever needed.

5- Now, whatever emotion is appearing, whether anger, frustration, impatience, rage, etc, have your angel say something like, *'are you ready to let this go?'*

6- Answer, yes, or no. Have your angel keep asking until you're no longer bothered by the situation.

7- Finally, thank your angel for bringing this thing to your attention.

As with the other examples and experiments in this book, this technique is simple. It does not require mountains of steps, confusing language, riddles or anything else.

Keep at this challenge. Introduce it to your daily routine. No one else needs to know what you are doing.

CHAPTER SEVEN

THE UNIVERSE IS WITHIN

The belief that we can change our lives, our circumstances, and even our world by looking within ourselves is not new. It's been around for millennia.

Enlightened and distinguished people throughout recorded history have said exactly that.

- Jesus - *"for behold, the kingdom of God is within you."* Luke 17:21

- Buddha - *"Change,'* the Buddha said, *'must come from within."*

- Lao Tzu – *"To the mind that is still, the whole universe surrenders."*

- Dalai Lama – *"When you realize that everything springs only from yourself, you will learn both peace and joy."*

- Gandhi - *"Be the change you wish to see in the world."*

○ Jiddu Krishnamurti – *"Look within, You are the world."*

- Rumi - *"There is a life-force within your soul, seek that life.*

  There is a gem in the mountain of your body, seek that mine.

  O traveler, if you are in search of That

  Don't look outside, look inside yourself and seek That."

○ Lester Levenson – *"The world is only an illusion that we created mentally. It is not external but in reality within us, within our mind. Someday you'll discover that you created this entire universe that you see."*

- Burt Goldman – *"Now then, what was it that was of such concern? Where is your trouble? Where is your problem? Where is the dilemma? It was a tale, only that; it signified nothing. The power was always, and only, within you."*

○ Marcus Aurelius - *"Very little is needed to make a happy life; It is all within yourself, in your way of thinking."*

- Dr Bruce Lipton – *"At one point, I realized that whenever I heard a negative conversation in my head, I needed to correct it right then, in that moment, and put in a more positive conversation… The beautiful part was that it didn't take very long before I started to realize that my life had turned around because I had changed my opinion of what I expected from my life. I started to become happier, healthier, and much more successful, not because the world had changed, but because I had changed."*

- Eckhart Tole – *"Those who have not found their true wealth, which is the radiant joy of being and the deep, unshakable peace that comes with it, are beggars, even if they have great material wealth. They are looking out-side for scraps of pleasure or fulfillment, for validation, security, or love, while they have a treasure within that not only includes all those things but is infinitely greater than anything the world can offer."*

- Robert Collier – *"With God like powers slumbering within, he is content to continue in his daily grind – eating, sleeping, working… The Power to be what you want to be, to get what you desire, to accomplish whatever you are striving for, abides within you."*

○ William Makepeace Thackeray – "*The world is a looking-glass and gives back to every man the reflection of his own face. Frown at it, and it will in turn look sourly upon you; laugh at it and with it, and it is a jolly kind companion.*"

Many others have stated that the true source of change comes only from within. Native American wisdom keepers have spoken of this.

"*Soon all their energy was used to protect themselves from the world around them, instead of making peace with the world within them.*" Gregg Braden

What the greats, the ancients, and the enlightened people of the past have said all along, is that to change, we must look within.

To look within, we must define what we mean by 'within', and how this relates to inspiring others.

WHAT AND WHERE *IS* 'WITHIN'?

So many people struggle with the idea of looking within for answers. On paper, the world within can appear a simple concept to understand, but with our current level of thinking, it becomes all twisted up and not so easy to implement.

Think of it this way: Your past and future are only thoughts you hold in mind. The past is your memories, the future, your desires. But they are not you. What you see in the world is a reflection of those thoughts you have held in mind and are holding in mind now. There are basically two worlds; the world out-there, and the world within.

Most of us it seems, think the world out there holds all the cards. If we get a great job with a high salary, a great house, a fancy car, a glowing relationship, a healthy family and a high-level education, then we have achieved success. Success has been given the label, '*Stuff*.' If we have stuff, then people will look upon us as successful.

We study different aspects of the world and the space surrounding it. We try to find the answers to almost every question imaginable by analyzing the human body, the earth, the water, the sky, space, time, planets, the sun, solar systems, our galaxy, and the universe. We have created a belief where the 'real world' is what we have studied and is all important. But by doing this, we are staring at the shadows in front of us, while ignoring where the shadows come from, as beautifully explained by Plato in *The Cave*. Any attempt in the past to turn around and announce to everyone else what is there, is met by anger and violence.

The world out there is a blanket covering the wonder and power of the world within. It is very effective at doing this. Who of us can resist the temptations of earning more, spending more, having the luxury most dream of but few experience?

While watching a video of Lester Levenson on a YouTube video recently, I heard him asking the participants of his seminar, '*why don't you do it?*" meaning, why don't you let go of all this pain. He answered this question by saying, You don't do it because you want the fame, the money, the big house and all the rest more than you want freedom.

What this means is, most people believe that by accumulating money, they *are* gaining freedom. They have the money to be free of the worry about where the next meal is coming from, or how to pay the bills. But what if the true source of abundance is not in how you conduct your life 'out there.' What if instead, by accepting and feeling the source of abundance as being within you, the world out-there changes to match that?

So How Does This Relate to Inspiring Others?

I've been doing this awhile, but I'm not one of those people who tried a system once, read part of a book, or watched a ten-minute video on YouTube, and POW, everything fell into the correct position, the planets aligned, and everyone lived happily ever after. So far, my progress has been a bit here, a bit there, and a whole lot of tripping up in between.

On many occasions I have sat down and meditated to quiet my mind. I've tried to focus on the now, and when I do it feels wonderful. Then my mind gets involved. I start thinking of that house I want, the landrover defender I want, the power

I want, and my thoughts go nuts. I think of what it would be like to have Jedi or X-men powers, to be able to heal people simply by pointing to them. By thinking of all the things I want from the world, I am saying to myself, I don't have them, I'm announcing I lack that and this, and the world out there wraps its long arms around me again and hands more lack to me.

One of the things I failed at in the past, is to move my thoughts from fear to action. I always believed I was an introvert. I believed I was incapable of standing up and offering my opinion to someone in case I offended them. This belief steered me away from the very thing I wanted to achieve, to inspire others. I allowed my past fears to control me.

How Coffee Shops Change the World?

To help overcome my fears, I asked a few close friends if they would like to meet at a local coffee shop. It was just a small group of two or three people. We got comfortable, drank coffee, and talked about our goals, and what we hoped to achieve in the coming months. We would focus on one member of the group at a time, talk about the barriers they faced, what their perspective was. Just by listening and bringing our opinions in, breaking things down into smaller bite sized pieces, we found that person lifted, energized and inspired. We simply provided encouragement to move past their fears and take action on a goal.

By doing this, you not only take that first step to inspire another, you also prove to yourself that inspiration comes easily, even from the smallest steps. You prove to yourself you *can* do it, and are as capable and effective at inspiring someone as anyone.

You can hold these casual meetings once a week, or every other week. Each time, you would hold one of the group accountable for their actions taken during the week. Only after everyone agrees that it's time to move on, would you focus on a different member of the group to inspire. Remember, everyone is being inspired whether they are the focus or not.

You don't have to use the word 'inspire', or 'inspiration' of course. Have your meeting and think of it as an action group. Give the group a name if it helps, '*Dare to Fail*', but use it to move someone forward in their thinking, in their goals and in their actions.

You will be amazed at how inspired you become by doing this. Your mind will start to see more opportunity everywhere. When you're walking down the street, eating lunch, talking to a friend, or while working. You become sensitized to seeking and finding solutions to people's problems. You also begin to see the barriers *you* have within you.

By focusing on things out there in the world, your world within can also change. Allowing your inspiring nature to flood up into your awareness will affect everything.

Start by getting a small group of friends together. You can use a physical location or a Facebook page or forum, the important thing is you meet regularly and have the intention to inspire. Give them a outline for the purpose of getting together. This isn't to chat about sports, or how life has thrown you a curve ball, it's about inspiring each group member by listening and discussing.

Focus on one person at a time. Digitally record the proceedings and write the relevant parts of the meeting down on paper. Use a journal to map out your journey (See 'What is a Gain Journal' in Chapter six). Bring it with you to the meeting so you can show everyone each little bit of success, each single step up the ladder.

Most of all, have a good time. Don't make it corporate or stressful, where the atmosphere is geared towards profit and nothing more. Keep this an enjoyable meeting of potential and transformation.

IF IT'S THIS SIMPLE, HOW COME THINGS STILL SUCK IN THE WORLD?

As we find in all areas of life, when things are going great, there's no incentive to keep moving up. Moving up takes commitment. Without commitment we often find ourselves at the bottom of the ladder before recognizing we're headed down. It all comes back to wanting the world more than we want inner freedom, meaning our egos are still in charge.

Changing what's going on within us is a step in the right direction, but it sometimes looks like the opposite is happening. We can get sidelined by thinking we're not moving in a forward direction.

I bring this up because I have often found myself meditating and going within but feeling that my world was caving in on me. I expected life to improve, not get worse, but a side effect of changing from within is that often, what you are suppressing, such as past fears, disapproval of yourself, or low self-esteem are brought up into your awareness. It feels like that more of these things are flooding into your life.

By focusing our intention on what we want, it may bring to light how the situation really is. It might appear things are getting worse. Whenever we begin a new fitness training regime for example, the first few times we work out, doesn't your body feel like you've been beaten with a large stick? But after a week or so of commitment and pushing through, the pain lessens, and you begin to feel the benefits of all the hard work. By being committed, you will become more peaceful and your mind will be clearer but only if you give things enough time.

> *"WHEN WE START LETTING GO OF THE EGO, IT APPEARS SOMETIMES AS IF THE EGO IS GETTING STRONGER AND STRONGER, BIGGER AND BIGGER. THAT'S NOT TRUE...WHAT HAPPENS IS THAT, AS WE LET GO OF IT, MORE OF IT PRESENTS ITSELF TO US."* LESTER LEVENSON

What we see 'out-there' is really not the issue. True change occurs from within. The world we see can and will change as long as we have the intention of changing it by changing ourselves within. If we bring enough people with us on this inner journey, the entire world out-there will change.

SEARCHING, ALWAYS SEARCHING

Searching for answers out there in the world is so easy to do. We get sucked in by advertising and images of what you can do with a boat load of money. We look for immediate pleasure in new jobs, new careers, new relationships, houses, cars, boats, clothes, jewelry, books, sport, booze, drugs, sex, movies, games, you name it. We do so to take away our pain. We create our problems through our thinking, then search elsewhere for the answers to those problems. You already have the answer to your problems, if you look in the right direction.

It's the perfect system, *if* you use it. The world really is the perfect opportunity to lift yourself, because by becoming aware of the stuff you are holding on to, you can let go of it all.

"THE REAL CHANGE HAPPENS BY BECOMING AWARE OF WHATEVER IS HAPPENING INSIDE YOU." ECKHART TOLLE.

I know I am emphasizing 'If you do it', because it's easy to look elsewhere for answers. Claims of *miracle products*, miracle *cure-alls*, the red pill brigade, flood our emails and the advertising airwaves every day. It's easy to get sucked in by the hype and fall into the 'grass is always greener' over there trap. But the answer still isn't out there.

It's not in those products, it never was. So much of what we think the world is, isn't. We have been duped into believing we have limited or no power at all. That takes some belief to accept I know. Intellectually I am sure many of us want to believe it, but our tendency is to buy a book, read it, get all excited by the possibilities, do some of the exercises, and then a short while later buy another book or course that says almost the same thing, it's just packaged better, or uses the words 'new age Jedi,' or 'wizard.'

Fortunately, over the last half century or so, science has begun to open up to a new way of thinking. Scientific research is finally backing up the claim that, *if you change what is going on within you, you change the world.*

There are now whole industries dedicated to the research, scientific analysis, and verification of the power of the world within. It is no longer thrown on the sci-fi garbage pile.

THE EVIDENCE

In the 1970s, a series of experiments by Dr David Orme-Johnson measuring the effects of consciousness on global events, (*The Journal of Conflict Resolution, 'International Peace Project in the Middle East,'*) showed remarkable and reproducible scientific results, that what we hold in mind can literally affect the world.

The Maharishi Experiment was conducted in order to show where '*the source of all conflict in society*' came from. The results were startling. Over a controlled period of time in the Lebanese village of Baskinta, a group of trained Transcendental Meditation researchers affected remarkable changes in the levels of violence, as compared to the surrounding areas by holding in mind only thoughts positivity and love.

The conclusion after several years of study was, *"stress in the collective consciousness of the nation and the world"* was the cause of violence and war.

The experiment showed that through the coming together of a small percentage of a population, all of whom adopt a unifying thought of love, we can change how the world works. This was a thoroughly researched and scientifically conducted experiment. (To see the full results from the Maharishi Experiment, see the Resource chapter.)

The reason for referencing this experiment is to show the connection between an en masse thought experiment and one-on-one inspiration. Both show an over-riding desire to help others first, and the results showcase the improvement of life circumstances in any area the experimentation or inspiration takes place.

In the Maharishi experiment, by holding love in their hearts and focusing on one area of the world, a more peaceful environment was brought about. Similarly, by seeking to inspire another, you lift them and yourself to a higher level within. In so doing, you are effecting a change in the world out there, it naturally becomes more inspired. The ramifications of either en-masse or individual inspiration are tremendous.

As we move towards a more connected society, our awareness will naturally filter through to others. Our personal level of freedom and connection to everyone around us will become more attuned and intense.

As the world is at present, we will be hard pressed to bring about peace while we hold fear, anger and hate within ourselves. Politicians will not bring about peace in one region of the world by offering peaceful policy, if they are talking war in another region. Only when we come together holding unconditional love within us will we see peace.

By holding love and peace in our hearts as much and as often as we can, we will slowly see hate and war lessen. The more of us who do this, the quicker we will impact and change the world.

THINK ABOUT THIS FOR A SECOND.

What you, and everyone around you hold in mind, right now, *can* actually affect what is happening in the world around you, and also in the world as a whole. By allowing love and inspiration for another to flow up, you overthrow the turmoil within, no matter what it is. You become more at peace, and the world becomes more peaceful.

You reflect onto the world what is happening within you!

What Are You Reflecting Now?

It's no secret that society has been very materialistic for quite a while. This isn't a criticism, or a judgment, it's just a fact. Very few people follow a path where 'things' and 'stuff' are weighed as less important than inner freedom. I am sure some reading this will fervently disagree, insisting that material objects hold little or no sway for them, and maybe I'm wrong, but all we have to do is turn on the television or computer and examine the evidence.

The truth is, we have been conditioned to believe the answer lies out there in a miracle product, in a new job, in a new house, or car, or a new partner, or new leader. We hold within us this belief that these things will help to make life better. By searching 'out there' for more and more stuff, we are essentially trying to fill the void within us, (created by our unhappiness at not 'being' our true unlimited self) because the stuff we continuously purchase and hold onto only gives us temporary relief from the hell out there. It doesn't solve the real problem because the real problem isn't out there, it's within us.

This is not fantasy or science fiction. This is not 'Star Wars', and I am not Obi Wan Kenobi, no matter how much I would like to be. Although what I've just said may appear negative, it is, as mentioned in chapter eight, an incredible opportunity for change.

Here is how I see the world.

Everything
that is happening in my life,
No matter what it is,
Everything,
is a mirror
of what is happening within me.

And it works the same for you.

Think about what most people hold in mind. What are you holding in mind right now?

All you have to do is look around at your life, the immediate life surrounding you.

What's happening in that space?

How does it feel?

If we broaden that view to encompass our country or in fact the entire world, take a look at the news on any television channel, and you will see what people hold in mind. Fear of almost everything and anything, so much so it would take multiple books just to list. Wants of control, wants of approval, of security, feelings of lack of this and that, lack of money, lack of love, frustrations, jealousy, hate and on and on.

Star Trek and the Mis-use of Emotion

"On the bridge, they had a last look at the *transcendence. It then became too lovely for them to comprehend, and so it was gone without ever really leaving.*

When Kirk began to relate to the here and the now of the Enterprise bridge, he turned to Spock. 'I wonder, did we just see the beginning of a new form of life out there?'

'Yes Captain. We witnessed a birth – perhaps also a direction in which some of us may evolve.'

'Only *some* of us, Spock?'

'It would seem to me, Captain, that the dimensions of creation make our future choices almost limitless.'

'It's been a long time since I helped deliver a baby,' said McCoy. "I hope we humans gave this one a good start.'

'I think we did,' Kirk answered. 'The Decker part of us gives it the ability to want and to enjoy, to hope and to dare and pretend and laugh.' Kirk smiled at his next thought. 'And the child will probably have some very interesting Deltan attributes, too. It should have an exciting future.'

McCoy gave a look toward Spock. 'And our other emotions? Fear, greed, jealousy, hate…?

'Those things are the *mis-use* of emotion, Doctor,' said Spock." Gene Roddenberry

Spock had it right, those *are* a '*mis-use* of emotion' because we are so powerful, but we casually throw that power aside, moaning, crying and complaining how bad we have it the whole time.

LISTENING TO OTHERS, LISTENING TO YOUR ANGELS

I have brought a lot of different aspects of living into this book. Letting go, being in the now moment, oneness, your angel guides. All of them are connected to each other. There is an underlying 'hand holding' going on between them. What I mean by this is, to inspire just one other person is to connect with everyone.

The act of inspiration is a selfless one, it brings each and every one of us closer together, but it also acts 'within' each of us. It connects you with your true self, the bigger picture so to speak. Every time you sit down and seek to inspire, you are dissolving negativities within you. You cannot avoid it even if you wanted to. That's what is so incredible about this.

Everything that occurs in your life,

From the loving, all the way to the most unpleasant,

All of this gives you access to your guide.

The loving will expand, and for everything else, your guide will *sing or scream* at you to change how you think about it.

Remember, this is your past thinking on display.

By acting on inspiration and listening to these guides, you let your past thinking out of the prison you built around it,

Which you must do because it will keep screaming at you until you listen.

By using inspiration to lift others up, you take charge as the warden of this prison. You are the one who is holding hostage all these feelings of limitation that you created in your past. Although they are hidden somewhere in your mind, they are still controlling what happens in your life, even now in this moment.

All you need do is listen. What happens is your little angel guide is constantly bringing things up into your awareness, so you can let them be free. Unfortunately, most of us *don't* listen.

You must try to realize that inspiration for example, is something inside of you. It is not out there in the world waiting for you to wander past and have an 'Aha' moment. That inspiration is already within you. It always has been and always will be.

If you are waiting to be inspired by a new dynamic form of leadership, or a new dynamic visionary, you are basically walking around like the 'see no evil, hear no evil,' character. You are blinding yourself from the opportunity that is within you just waiting. It is patiently waiting, wondering why you don't use it, asking, 'Why are you searching for something you already have? It's right here.'

By accessing your inspiration from within, you realize the world really is your oyster. You realize all of a sudden, what is truly available to you, and that nothing is dependent on what happens 'out-there.'

Your life is what you make it. Your power is within you, right now, in this moment. Arjuna Ardagh spoke of the 'Now' moment in The Translucent Revolution. "*We discover that there is no such thing as past or future; we need thought to create them. You have no childhood unless you think of it. Next Christmas does not exist, except in thought. All that can really be known for real, without thinking, is this moment.*"

You now understand why the economy has no power over you, why it's no longer that merciless ruler of your fortunes, why politicians no longer hold power over how, or what, where, and when you live your life. All the power, love, peace, happiness is within you in this moment, now.

If you let go of something such as a fear, it no longer has power over you, and will no longer affect the world around you. Your fear within will no longer reflect on to the world out there. You will be free of it. You can achieve this by inspiring others.

If Enough of Us Do This, We Can Change the World

Do you realize what an opportunity this is?

Everything is laid out right in front of you, right in front of all of us. It's like the dinner bell has gone off…

The evidence has been there all along, we've just been looking in the wrong direction. Science is slowly realizing the truth of that claim, even if it's kicking and screaming the whole way.

We (as oneness) hold the universe within us. If we look within, we will find

> "*TODAY'S PHYSICISTS HAVE COMPLETELY FAILED TO INFORM THE PUBLIC OF THE PURELY MENTAL NATURE OF THE UNIVERSE.*" Dr Bruce Lipton.

what we hold in mind, we will find why our lives and the world are the way they are.

Every thought you held on to in your past affects and creates your world now. I know how scary that can seem but it's also empowering. It hands you the keys to your life. You put those thoughts in, but you can change your thoughts. By changing *them*, you change your world. By helping others to change their views, their thinking, you lift yourself up, which changes your view and your thinking. (Sometimes it is easier to advise others than listen to your own advice.)

This idea allows you to access subconscious thoughts and free them. So, does this require anything other than inspiring a friend?

Yes.

The whole process requires one important aspect, commitment. That's it. You must be committed to doing this, otherwise it will fall by the wayside like most new year's resolutions.

Think about this, we have been handed the keys to the universe millennia ago but we still fall off the wagon and struggle. This is one of the true jewel encrusted secrets of all, and again, it's not a secret. I have mentioned in other areas of this book, that this information has been openly available, written down again and again, and this raises a giant question.

Why, if this magnificent power is so easily accessed, why don't we make use of it?

One reason is, we have been programmed not to believe it. We rarely believe something so powerful and life influencing is free to all and this simple to use. But it is this simple, and can be made even more simple by making it happen in the life of another.

"The Kingdom of God is inside you and all
around you,
Not in a mansion of wood and stone.
Split a piece of wood and I'm there,
Lift a stone and you will find me."
From the movie 'Stigmata'

SUMMARY

The world within is a reflection, a mirror image of the world out there. Some will hate on this idea as it suggests blame, but what it really does is hand us the keys to the universe. It gives us access to total freedom.

If you listen to your angel guides, tapping on your shoulder, you will soon realize how blessed you are. Each moment really becomes an opportunity.

To inspire one other person is to connect with everyone. The act of inspiration is a selfless one, bringing every one of us closer together. It also acts within each of us. It connects you with your true self.

Every time you sit down and seek to inspire someone else without expecting or wanting anything in return, you dissolve negativities within you.

In the following chapter 'On Air Broadcasting', you will understand that every thought you have is transmitted to everyone else. You are broadcasting your inner personality all the time. This isn't something to be scared of, in fact, it empowers you even more. You become more of an inspiration.

MY FOURTH CHALLENGE TO YOU.

Have you ever noticed, when you smile at others how it changes their attitudes? A simple smile is powerful. I Challenge all reading this to smile with genuine happiness and love in your heart at as many people as you can for a week, especially grumpy people, and see how you can change them.

I have a close friend called Don who is a perfect example of this challenge. When people ask him how he is doing, he always replies with a bright loving smile, '*wonderful, because I have Jesus in my life.*' Some non-religious people may be surprised at first, but then they feel a deep, positive, heart-felt greeting and the warm genuine care coming from Don, and they become lifted from wherever they are. Then they respond in the same or a similar manner. It's not just about his cowboy hat.

Warning: This challenge may appear simple, but it can have tremendous impact on you and those you smile at. It will single you out from the crowd. It *will* bring you more attention.

CHAPTER SIX

'ON AIR' BROADCASTING

You have your own 'TV Show' going out right now. Congratulations.

Did you know that?

You are broadcasting your inner self out to the world in every moment.

We are all broadcasting our own tv shows out to the world. We do it all the time, every single second, we're just not aware of it.

This show is called the, '*This is what I really think of me*' show. It's your internal view of 'You,' that deep down feeling that you sense about your-self. It's where your show is created. This show is going out into the world now, and everyone is picking up on it.

SO, WHAT *ARE* YOU BROADCASTING TO THE WORLD?

I remember walking in to a pub in London years ago with four friends. We had come up by train to go out and have a good time in the big city. We were excited by the prospect as all of us came from a small town and rarely did we venture outside our comfortable surroundings.

The train came in to Liverpool street station and within about ten minutes we had found a pub that suited us. From the outside it displayed an old-world character with lots of bright lights and a busyness we were hoping for but as we walked in, all five of us were hit hard by the awful stench of negativity.

It was such a thick sickening feeling that before we had reached the bar, all of us turned around and walked out. I felt physically ill by the time I got outside, no more than ten steps. It felt violent, hateful and soul draining in that place.

I remember saying to my friends how I thought we had almost fallen through the gates of hell.

What we experienced that night was an accumulation of feelings from everyone, or nearly everyone in that pub. It was probably their hangout, as I cannot for the life of me think how anyone else could have ventured within and endured such torture.

My inner signal, the one I am broadcasting is dependent on my beliefs about me. I'm quiet, I'm shy, I'm loud, I'm frustrated, I'm stupid, I'm too smart, I'm inferior, I'm not funny, and many more.

Changing your external world makes little difference to your beliefs about yourself and the signal you broadcast unless it directly affects you within. Being an inspiration, having thoughts about how to lift another person has the effect of altering the signal you broadcast. You start to believe in yourself.

COMPOUND INSPIRATION

"How can compassion be good for you when you're sacrificing, exposing yourself to vulnerabilities?

One of the ways compassion can be strong is it contagiously spreads to other people so that they'll feel compassion, right? Then you've got this little network of people feeling compassion and more likely to share and cooperate.

And there are really neat studies to show that compassion is contagious. We know this intuitively but it's good to have the science to back it up. So, if I give some resources to you, let's say I volunteer for you to help you out, you are moved by my generosity and kindness, you are more likely to give resources to the next person you interact with, even if I'm not there, and then that person is more likely to give resources to the next person she or he interacts with." Dacher

Kelter Phd Professor of Psychology University of California, Berkley.

That study is the same reasoning behind *Your* Inspiration is Needed. We want to inspire one, to inspire another, to inspire another. We can call this inspirational compassion, or compound inspiration. By inspiring without wanting anything in return, we actually get far more out of this than we could imagine.

First, we are lifting ourselves, our belief in ourselves, our self-purpose. We are changing within. Second, as mentioned by Professor Kelter in the above quote, by inspiring another, who inspires another, who inspires another, the energy is compounded as the inspiration spreads. It becomes community felt.

When large groups of people come together with the same intention, the energy within each member of that group is enhanced and multiplied by the other members. This is how this all works.

We are feeding love, compassion, inspiration, positive energies into the community. With more people coming on board, that energy field builds. A vibrant, radiant transformative potential is created, as in the Maharishi Effect. It spreads out like ripples on water after a pebble is dropped in, then another is dropped in, and another.

You see this at seminars where the accumulated energy from the people there is electric. The energy high is like the feeling you get at a live rock concert compared to sitting in your living room listening to a cd. It builds and builds like the workings of an atomic explosion. A change is felt within. It is amplified. These ripples spread out across the entire expanse of water, continually fueled by ripples from more pebbles.

The effect on the world can be miraculous.

The result out there in the world is created by the accumulation of thought intentions held on to.

How can you keep hold of, and amplify positive thoughts? One way is to Use a Gain Journal.

WHAT IS A GAIN JOURNAL?

A gain journal is a very simple tool to show your progress, but it has other more powerful attributes hiding at the edge of the stage behind the curtain.

The basics of a gain journal is just that, a journal. It is there for you to write in every evening what you have gained from the day.

"Today, I felt frustrated when I got to work. The drive in sucked and took longer than usual because of traffic. Nothing seemed to be working how I like, but I caught myself. I saw how this attitude was only going to make me more and more miserable. I sat there and took a minute to breathe deeply, then I let this anger come up and said to it, 'I love you'. After doing this for a few minutes, I felt totally different. My outlook changed. I went about with the purpose of making life as wonderful and inspiring for my

fellow workers as I could. I felt like I was making a difference. It was like coming alive for the first time."

This is an example of a gain, or in this case several gains. By writing these down, documenting them, you give them a voice. You are acknowledging the gain.

I did say there were other powerful attributes from using a gain journal.

THE FIRST IS MOMENTUM

By writing your gains each evening, you are creating momentum and habit. Many times, we have good intentions of staying fit, changing our diet, drinking less, that kind of thing, but unless we create a plan and document it for a minimum period of time, we often fall off the wagon and go back to our old habits. The gains process is no different. Documentation when you first begin is essential to continuity. The more you write down your gains, the more natural it becomes. You gain by doing it, which brings us to the most powerful attribute of all:

THE SECOND IS EXPANSION

The more you write down your gains, the more gains you will notice in your life. They may be small gains to start, but the effect of noticing and acknowledging them can be dramatic on your outlook. Your thinking will begin to change. You suddenly start to see how fulfilled and amazing your life really is. Gains start turning up everywhere, small, medium and even large ones. The more you document your gains, the more you notice gains all around you. You begin to welcome in more of it, and more gains begin to show up in your life.

Gain journals are another example of a process that is so simple but so effective. The simplicity of it is I believe the reason you do not see this around every corner of business and personal life: People think if it's too simple, it probably doesn't work.

A BENEFIT RARELY SPOKEN OF

Another benefit of using a Gain Journal is it gives you a positive framework, a foundation to fall back on when you lose the high. So let me explain what I mean by that, because this is one of those issues rarely brought up regarding inspirational seminars, coaching, or any area of life where you can get lifted up by the surrounding energy.

At any seminar you attend, there is a tendency to get swept away by all the opportunity, the promises, and hope. The natural energy is usually high, if facilitated by a real professional. But what happens *after* the event?

I have been to a good number of seminars on all sorts of topics. Real Estate, Alternative Health,

Motivation. When I leave the auditorium, I'm buzzing with energetic determination. I go home and make all these plans. I try to set things up, and what I find is, the direction I hoped to zoom down is now filled with hurdles, barriers, and choked with confusing smog. I have lost my high and my direction.

This is where a Gain Journal comes in. The simple act of continually documenting any gains (most of the time small ones at the beginning), allows you to get past the loss of your high. It provides you with the impetus to sweep away the obstacles that were put back up after your high, because you can see (from the gains) that you are still moving in a forward direction.

That is an important part of this, to keep moving forward. Realizing this is essential.

So many of us give up on an idea, or a course of work because we don't feel progress. It's probably there but we usually expect explosive results, like the results we were told about at the seminar. A Gain Journal will focus you on the positives, no matter what is happening around you.

Over Complication

Humans have an annoying and irrational habit of over complicating things. In the process, they become less direct, confusing, and in many cases, create more stress than they're supposed to solve.

One area you see this all the time is politics. Now, I'm not getting in to the whole political scene but it would seem we over complicate matters to make ourselves appear to be in control, to sell an idea and stoke our egos at the same time.

If someone can make a simple answer appear complicated and confusing to others, such as when an attorney explains the details of a legal document, a feeling of control over the person listening, can occur. In this example, the attorney might feel it gives them power, but it is ego power only. This power rarely helps anyone.

> *"SIMPLICITY IS HARD TO BUILD, EASY TO USE, AND HARD TO CHARGE FOR. COMPLEXITY IS EASY TO BUILD, HARD TO USE, AND EASY TO CHARGE FOR."* CHRIS SACCA INVESTOR AND ENTREPRENEUR.

SIMPLICITY IS POWER

The more simple and direct something is, the more powerful and effective it can be.

When looking at a situation, or the complexities we have shrouded the world in through the eyes of a child, it can be illuminating. *"Look at everything always as though you were seeing it either for the first or last*

> *"CHILDHOOD MEANS SIMPLICITY. LOOK AT THE WORLD WITH THE CHILD'S EYE - IT IS VERY BEAUTIFUL."* KAILASH SATYARTHI

time: Thus is your time on earth filled with glory." Betty Smith.

Problem solved!

It's an obvious solution but we tend to disregard or look past such simple solutions purely because we have been taught to do so. But this habit can be turned around and everyone can benefit from doing it. The more simple your life becomes, the easier it will be to navigate. Dr Richard Bartlett explained this in his book, The Physics of Miracles.

"When we measure, most of us judge what we are measuring. We try to analyze it. We try to make sense of it. We try to make it mean something that fits our perception of the way the real world functions. There is something called innocent perception. Innocent perception or practicing the patterns of perception means that you notice whatever shows up. Our path of expectation assumes that there is a cause and effect to things: that if we do this, then this will happen, and if we do not, then something else will happen. There is no logic to it. But it is a logic we have embraced."

We have convinced ourselves the more complicated a process, the better and more expensive it will and can be. It is the exact opposite of truth.

When I was young, my father told me about a theory he had regarding the halo often seen in depictions of Jesus. He suggested that the halo may in fact have been a clear space helmet. My father is a scientist and so I did not see him as someone likely to suggest such an idea on a whim, a flight of fancy so to speak.

Whether there is any truth to this or not, is not relevant here. It is just an example of a simple theory from my past, producing a different perspective on a popular view of Christ depicted in most pictures.

To give another example of how another person or person's perspective can influence us, comes from my past and revolves around my health. (I *would* say, 'when I was young' but the perspective I will mention continues to this day.)

At the age of seven I was diagnosed with type one diabetes. From the moment I was hospitalized, almost every doctor (and I have seen many doctors) have told me as a matter of unarguable fact that, '*what you have is incurable*,' and/or '*you will have it for the rest of your life*.' The simple way to look at this (from my perspective) is to ask, '*is this truth, or have I been programmed to believe this?*'

At first, I did not ask this of myself. I was seven after all. It was years later I began to question the truth of the statements made.

By asking this question, I have come to one conclusion: I do not believe 'incurable' exists. No one doctor knows of all the medical cures or alternative methodologies after all. They don't know what discoveries will occur within the next day, week, month or year. This is an example of how systematic programming over-rides simplicity. I will not go into the ramifications of our programmed society except to say, this shows how influenced and limited we have become, purely because we accept what we are told. We accept the delusion of complexity over simplicity, and often for financial gain.

For thousands of years, the real answers to problems such as the one mentioned above (diabetes), have been announced again and again on the side lines of mainstream thinking, but are often pushed aside as too simplistic, or just ridiculous. We can suggest this is to control the masses, but the point is, we have labelled people who view the world in these simplistic ways as simpletons, using the term in a negative fashion.

The real truth is, simplicity is clarity, and clarity is power.

In the world of advertising, a complicated or clever message in an advert is considered the work of an amateur. No good copywriter will do it. (You do see it all the time in television advertising, but it is mostly put together by agencies who go under the assumption (not results) that to sell, you must entertain, you must be clever and witty).

If we break down a system into its smallest parts, we see simplicity at work. Our desire to over-complicate is based solely on our desire for control.

By understanding the power of simplicity, the broadcast you put out to the universe becomes more and more clear. The fog will gradually lift around your thoughts and the path forward will become obvious. Your broadcast to anyone you are sitting down with, talking to about their future and their dreams, will assist you in creating belief in them about what they can achieve.

WHAT IS OUR BIGGEST OBSTACLE TO TAKING THE LEAP?

There are certainly many contenders for the number one spot, but one always tops the rest. It is the thing that stops abundance in its tracks, holds back adventure, crushes love and even twists beliefs from flowing freely. It is the single most toxic element of life and we have given free rein to it.

We now live our lives on an intertwining helix with this thing. It has become part and parcel of our everyday make up, and incredibly, we both love and hate it. But it slivers and slides into every aspect of our lives, controlling, deciding, and masking our true wants and the roads to happiness.

What is it?

If you haven't already figured it out, here it is:

Fear.

Fear is the killer of dreams, hopes, goals, desires, opportunities, potential, partnerships, and breakthroughs. It is the reason for failure and the inability to bounce back from failure. And at some point, it knocks on the door of everyone, sometimes disguised as your best friend or guiding angel.

Fear may appear at first to be an uncontrollable and unconquerable foe, but if that were the case, we as humans would rarely have achieved anything. So what can the average person do to use fear to their advantage and conquer such a challenging beast?

I HAVE A FEW IDEAS TO HELP

1- **Breathe**. Yes, it's obvious but it's also effective. Take a deep slow breath in through your nose, a velvety smooth breath and let it out through your mouth. Keep focusing on your breathing. Do this for a couple of minutes or so.

2- **Find a quiet space** and close your eyes. Allow your mind to go quiet. Any thoughts that come in, just let them pass by. Focus on your breathing as in the above example. Do this for ten minutes.

3- **Find the 'Now' moment**. Focus your attention on 'now'. This is a strange thing to do because most of us live in our memories (past) or desires and fears (future). Try to do this while taking a walk. Think to yourself, each moment is a miracle unfolding.

4- **Change your perspective**. Realize that when you become aware of a fear rising up from within, it is your guiding angel taping you on the shoulder saying, *'you need to let go of this.'*

5- **Change the way you look at your fears**. Instead of retreating from fear, look upon fear as an exciting new 'Indiana Jones' style adventure. Fear is an incredible opportunity for you. When you feel fear, it is 'Opportunity' being handed to you, right where you are.

Relish the idea of jumping in head first. Use the fear to build a fire within and stoke the fire to lift you up. Remember, your fears are just thoughts you had in the past and have held on to.

SUMMARY

You are a broadcasting station. Every thought you have is sent out and picked up by everyone else. Scary isn't it? But this is a giant opportunity, not something to be feared.

Have you ever met someone and before either of you had even spoken, you felt like old friends? Or the opposite, you could hardly stand being near them?

I had a friend a few years ago called Mark W. I was first introduced to Mark by another friend at a pub in a town called Sleaford in Leicestershire, England. I can honestly say, I immediately felt like I had known him all my life, and we got on as if we had. It was a connection before either of us said a word. This would seem to be an unusual event, and I have thought of it as such for years, but it happens all the time, to everyone, we just don't acknowledge it.

The personality you feel within you, is the one everyone else senses. Again, don't fear this. As you change within, you broadcast the new you to the world. It might seem like the scary monster under the bed, but because you have become aware of it, you have gained control of it. It is now in your power to change what is being broadcast. Try and look at everything the way Ralph Waldo Emerson saw things: *"See the miraculous in the common."* That is real power.

Use a Gain Journal to document your journey. The more you do this, the more you will recognize opportunities when they are presented to you.

In the following chapter 'Core Values', I will share with you my eight guiding principles (my core values), and how, by writing down your guiding principles, it can help you stay on track and soar to heights you never realized were possible.

MY FIFTH CHALLENGE TO YOU

I have been using a specific motivational technique since I became the 'Sergeant at Arms' at my local Toastmasters club, 'Cleveland County Communicators' in Shelby North Carolina in October 2016.

I do not remember where I got the idea for this technique from, except that I used a lesser version of it when I was younger to energize myself when I felt small, scared or intimidated.

It's simple, (once again), and works like magic. It's also loud.

So, what is this technique?

I call it 'The Lions Roar'.

When I have stood up to open a meeting, the best thing I can do is boost the energy in the room. The bigger the crowd, the better. But on occasion, (actually quite often), those who have joined me in the Roar have been a little shy of letting down their guard and bringing up that ferocious lion within them.

I understand this. It can be intimidating.

My own experiences with this technique showed me how scared I was of being loud. I first practiced my 'big' Roar at my house when my wife and son were out, giving me free rein to burst my lungs. How difficult could it be after all. But even in an empty house, my BIG Roar, was more of a cat's meow. I was conscious of what the neighbors would think if they heard me. Maybe they would think I had injured myself, or was savaging the computer in a mad fit of rage?

It took me several attempts before I really surrendered, let go, and opened up to the full power within me. My advice is to take baby steps.

So here it is:

1- Decide if you will do this alone, or in a small group. (Small groups are a great way to start.) It is also best to do this on a relatively empty stomach.

2- If you are alone but still cannot be too loud, (apartments, condo's, coffee shop) you can try a silent or quiet Roar. It can be done but you will need to use the full capability of your gut.

3- Your intention in this challenge should be to explode from the inside out. Let it all up, the passion, the emotions, the desires, the love, bring it all out in a single soul lifting volcanic explosion. Your stomach should feel the tremors from your Roar. Your abs should violently tighten like someone is about to punch you in the gut, thrusting the molten core of all you've held within for so long upwards and out. It wants to come out. It wants to erupt and expand.

4- So take a few deep breaths. Really feel your stomach, then your chest expanding each time.

5- Then one more deep breath in, grip your abdominal muscles and Roar like your life depended on it. Don't hold anything back. Roar for as long and as loud as you can.

You will feel so alive after you've done this. The ripples from this explosion will spread through you, energizing areas you'd forgotten you had. You will feel ready to take on almost anything.

I challenge you to let your Roar flood out. Let the world finally hear from you.

As stated above, this technique is even more pronounced and energizing in a group setting. The more the merrier.

CHAPTER FIVE

CORE VALUES

WHAT ARE CORE VALUES?

Core values show how you want to live your life. They are a guide if you find you are losing your way. They can help to correct your direction, to set yourself back on the path based on what is most important to you.

HOW YOUR CORE VALUES HELP TO INSPIRE OTHERS?

It surprises me how few people write down what is most important to them. Yes, we hold these values in our heart but because life is such a fast paced, chaotic and often stressful thing, even our most heartfelt feelings and values can get lost. It sometimes feels like we're all walking around in a thick fog, feeling our way through our lives when all the time we can just breath our values out into this fog and disperse it to show the path.

The values most important to you will help with the clarity by which you inspire others. To them, you will appear far more in control when you know what is most important to you. Let's face it, most people struggle with what they want to achieve in life. By holding to a set of guidelines, (those heartfelt values you believe in,) you will rise above the average person. The inspiration and advice you give because of it, will be profound.

YOUR VALUES ARE YOURS ALONE

We all have a number of paths we would like to follow. Some maybe based around work, (what we truly want to accomplish in our chosen field), others will be of a more spiritual nature, based upon our beliefs about life, the universe, and if we think there is more to ourselves than we are told in school.

Whatever your values are, they are *your* beliefs, *your* pathways, and are important to you. If you share them with someone else, don't be surprised, or disheartened, if you find yourself pushed to defend them.

Don't.

Everyone will have slightly different paths. I believe these paths all lead to the same destination in the end, but why argue or become frustrated if someone disagrees with the route you feel best to take. It's a waste of your time.

I have travelled across the United States many times. My wife and I have lived a semi-nomadic life in a lot of states and a few more temporary ones in between. Our trend was to set up shop on one side of the country and then move it all to the other side.

From North Carolina we went to Colorado, then back, then we moved to Alaska, then to Maryland. From there we went to Washington state, and back to North Carolina. I drew out a map of our trips. We took I-90 in the North, I-70 in the middle, I-40 in the South and moved between them, up and down searching for those things along the routes which interested us the most at the time. (See 'The Map' in chapter nine.)

There was 'The Little Big Horn' in Montana, Devil's Tower in Wyoming, the Meteor crater near Winslow in Arizona, the Grand Canyon, Yellowstone National Park, 'Wall Drug' in Wall, South Dakota, the corn palace in Mitchell, South Dakota, all of these had special meaning to us.

Some of these routes are faster, less cluttered, while others are more beautiful and serene but slower. What is most important, is whichever route you take it is taken because of the value to the driver. Whichever your route, it is not wrong.

Your core values are those places/attractions/ monuments along your inner route. They show you the way on the map of life.

Is it hard to stick to your core values?

When you write your core values down, you may feel pressured to hold to them at all costs. '*If I don't stick to them, I've failed*'. Just remember what they really are. They are your own set of guidelines. Their purpose is to help you when you feel a bit lost. Your heart GPS so to speak. They are not rules. There is nothing to break, no consequences, they are just guiding lights. They can give you a sense of purpose.

My number three core value (as you will see later in this chapter), is something I try to feel within me. '*I will be positive and loving no matter what is going on around me.*' I try to hold this in my heart as often as I can because it feels so wonderful when I do. It guides me back to the light. But I still find myself acting otherwise now and then. When this happens, my angel guide gives a little cough, '*ah hem*,' then whispers in a soft caring way, '*that's not very loving.*'

The great thing is, once I realize I am not being all loving and positive, no matter the situation, I know I can change. I can release those feelings and actions of negativity and set myself free from those binding/enslaving thoughts. I do my best to allow that to come out. I can invite it up from wherever it is within me and set it free.

Now, like everyone else, I tend to beat myself up during times of stress, and wonder '*What the hell is the matter with me?*' It's afterwards that I realize I have not stuck to my core values.

What do you do in these situations?

Let me ask you this?

Does it help to berate yourself?

Do you feel good if you bring yourself down and say, '*how could I be so stupid?*'

Do you feel better after doing it?

No, of course not. No one has ever felt better by beating ourselves up.

Whenever you are being a bear to yourself, step away from wherever you are, take a deep breath, and use a very simple method to help.

(It may seem too simple to some of you but has the power of a giant if you use it.)

Start to focus on your 'in' breath, and 'out' breath. Keep this focus going, then begin to say (either silently or out loud) '*Yes*'. That's all. (See 'Releasing' in the resource chapter for further details about how to expand this method.)

Keep this going. '*Breath in, Yes, Breath out, Yes, Breath in, Yes.*' Your 'Yes' will get louder within you. You will suddenly find yourself smiling. You may be thinking, '*this is so stupid,*' but you will find after a short while you are laughing out loud.

It is simple, but it is extremely effective.

To give you an example of core values, I have included my own top eight here.

MY CORE VALUES

1-I believe everyone and everything is part of one thing. That there is no separation between us and God. We are all a part of, and one with God.

2-Darkness is not a place to fear, or a place to show your fist to God. Just be thankful you have been given the opportunity to be a light in that darkness.

3-I will be positive and loving no matter what goes on around me.

4-I am a representation of the divine. Just demonstrate in action who I am.

5-Everything I am searching for, I already am. Search within and I will find the answers.

6-If I knew I could not fail, what would I do? Ask this question often.

7-Everything happening in the world is a reflection of what is happening within me. Use what is happening in the world to let go of my attachments to it.

8-I am driven by the idea that anything negative is within, and can simply be let go of. There are no exceptions to this.

As stated in the previous chapter, be careful not to disregard simplicity just because it is simple. By disregarding something because of simplicity, you can potentially destroy the opportunity.

Many times, we look at a simple explanation, or simple solution and disregard it. We allow ourselves to be influenced by the believe that complex is always better. Don't be fooled. The simplicity of writing down your core values will become self-evident in all areas of your life almost before the ink has dried.

SUMMARY

Core values are your guiding principles in life. When the life you have dreamt about appears to slide into a feeling of stuckness, your core values can help lift the fog, giving you clarity once again.

Knowing what your core values are can help you when talking with someone. You will be able to relate back to the person you hope to inspire with your values keeping you on track. You will appear so much more composed and understanding of the principles of life by mapping out those things that mean the most to you.

The purpose of writing them down is so they become a fixed part of your day, no matter what goes on. By doing this, they become cemented into the fabric of your life and will help to guide and direct you in harder times.

If you have not jumped in to the challenge above, I urge you to do so now.

Write down your top five (at least your top five) Core Values. Read them out loud to yourself every day. You'll be surprised how this simple under-rated step can transform you.

Imagine having your most heartfelt beliefs as your guiding light when helping another. Imagine how centered you will become even in stressful situations with this simple tool beside you. This is something that will help in so many areas of life, personal, business and spiritual. It is a miracle it's not taught in school.

In the following chapter 'You don't have to be inspiring to be inspirational', we will address the elephant in most people's room. '*How can I inspire someone else, when I can't even inspire myself?*' Everyone has this fear at first, but don't be put off. Inspiration is not always what it seems.

MY SIXTH CHALLENGE TO YOU

If you have not done it already, I suggest you go and get a sheet of paper and pen, or turn on your computer to a word document, and begin to think about what *Your* Core Values are.

Take your time doing this. It is an important step. Remember, these are *Your* values, *Your* guides. No one else comes in to it or needs to be involved. It does not matter what anyone else thinks or believes, and you do not have to show these to anyone, ever, if you don't want to.

Make sure *Your* Core Values resonate within you. You will feel how important they are to you as you think about them.

So here is the challenge:

I challenge you to think about what *Your* Core Values are, and then write them down as clearly as you can. Write as many as feels right to you.

If it takes you a week, or even a month to get them down, that's fine, that's perfect. Just make sure you do it.

CHAPTER FOUR

YOU DON'T HAVE TO BE INSPIRING TO BE INSPIRATIONAL

"One of the commonest mistakes and one of the costliest is thinking that success is due to some genius, some magic — something or other which we do not possess. Success is generally due to holding on, and failure to letting go. You decide to learn a language, study music, take a course of reading, train yourself physically. Will it be success or failure? It depends upon how much pluck and perseverance that word "decide" contains. The decision that nothing can overrule, the grip that nothing can detach will bring success. Remember the Chinese proverb, "With time and patience, the mulberry leaf becomes satin."
— Maltbie Davenport Babcock

I worked from home when I wrote this book. My wife and I (mostly her) homeschooled our son Hans, who as a young child (4ish on) displayed a lot of anger. At times, when I was writing about 'Oneness', or about 'Beingness', and looking within to use the issues in the world as a guiding angel, our son would blow up, my wife would become frustrated and blow up, and I would become frustrated in my little office upstairs, listening to what was going on, saying to myself, *'this anger is in me… could I let it go… use this negativity as my guiding angel, just quiet your mind,'* blah, blah, blah, *'will you please keep it down/ be quiet/ what the hell is going on'* etc., and then I would beat myself up for losing it.

I hardly acted as I suggest in this book. How could I write about inspiring others to greatness, about looking within for the answers, when I couldn't lift my own son from the darkness surrounding him?

YOU CAN DO THIS BECAUSE I CAN DO THIS

I have a Bachelor of Science degree in Archaeology, and a Master of Science degree in Osteology and Palaeopathology. I have written 3 books to date with 2 more in the works. I have worked in some of the most dangerous and extreme places in the world, yet I have felt less qualified, less experienced, less knowledgeable and less competent than those in the same or similar professions.

I have believed in the past that I would be below average in an IQ test. I have put my degrees down to luck, and the positions I have held as examples of those hiring me not knowing who I was and falsely believing I was smart, (maybe due to my accent.) I'm an Englishman, which seems to get me an extra 10 or 20 IQ points.

All of this relates to self-esteem. It relates to my belief in who I am. It is only since writing my books that I have addressed this by changing the way I think, and releasing my past thoughts, and self-limiting beliefs.

Most people out there would like to be better than they think they are. Most people look at the big names, the actors, the tv show hosts, the great talkers, comedians, artists, the motivators, and great inspirational leaders and believe, '*I could never do that*'.

But why shouldn't you do it?

What's stopping you from doing what the big names are doing, except you do it *your* way?

There is only one answer to this. It's '*You.*' It's you thinking you can't. That's what is stopping you. That's the *only* thing stopping you. Nothing else comes in to it.

EXERCISE:

Get out your Gain Journal and document why you believe you cannot do something. Write it down and take a good look at what you are holding in mind.

So, what *are* you thinking right now?

'*I'm not the motivating type.*'

'*I can't inspire myself let alone someone else.*'

'*I'm not a leader, people won't follow me.*'

'*Tony Robbins already does this, who would listen to me, I'm nobody.*'

Any of those sound familiar? I've heard them all because I wrote this book.

I understand what you're thinking. You may not have done this kind of thing before, at least not seriously. But remember what you just wrote down about yourself. You told yourself all the reasons you can't do it. *That* is the reason you can't, not your lack of experience in this field or in life.

Stop thinking you have to be Tony Robbins to do this.

EXERCISE:

Write down in your Gain Journal what you see success is in your chosen field.

What do you believe is in your way, and/or stopping you from getting to that point?

What is the gap between where you are now, and where you want to be?

Be honest with this exercise. No one else has to read what you write down. Your Gain Journal will benefit only you, so be as open with yourself as you can.

Remember, by doing this, you begin to understand what is influencing you, and therefore what's stopping you from reaching the level of success you dream of.

I said earlier that it took Tony Robbins years to get where he is now. The reason he's where he is now, is because he took those first steps.

He spoke to one person on the street with a basic message. Then another, and another. Then two people, and it grew over a long time. Without those first steps, no one goes anywhere. It takes time to build charisma and presence and be inspirational, not because it takes time but because we believe it takes time. We accept that as a natural process, and that's okay. Don't be put off by it, but you still need to take the first step.

Robert Collier wrote in his book, Riches Within Your Reach, "*The Declaration of Independence starts with the preamble that all men are born free and equal.*

But how many believe that? When one child is born in a Park Avenue home, with doctors and nurses and servants to attend to his slightest want, with tutors and colleges to educate him, with riches and influence to start him in his career, how can he be said to be born equal to the child of the ghetto, who has difficulty getting enough air to breathe, to say nothing of food to eat, and whose waking hours are so taken up with the struggle for existence that he has no time to acquire much in the way of education!

Yet in that which counts most, these two are born equal, for they have equal access to the God in themselves, equal chance to give means to his expression. More than that, the God in one is just as powerful as the God in the other."

We all have this access because the universe *is* within us.

EXERCISE:

So here is one more Gain Journal entry for you.

Choose a goal, or a dream, or an interest you have. Something that keeps ringing the bell in your mind, but for some reason you have never moved on it or taken action on it.

Write down (as a hypothetical exercise) how you would do it *Your* way.

Forget how it has been done up to now. Be as outrageous as you need to be to get that goal, dream, interest accomplished. Go into details. Break this thing in to small bite sized pieces, and see how you can make it work, and how you can make it happen.

Remember, this is a hypothetical exercise, so your level of money, or power or any of those things is irrelevant.

This is an exercise in expansion. You will find your ideas will expand and may even show you how this goal, dream, interest can *actually* be possible.

How a Little Plant Can Change the World

Dr Win Wenger (winwenger.com) developed Image Streaming. It is a method whereby you ask a question, then get your conscious mind distracted, allowing a subconscious answer to come up in to your awareness.

When I first image streamed, my question was, what is the most important aspect of my book I need to focus on? I assumed the answer would be clear, straight forward, and even written down for me to study. I was wrong.

My quest for an answer began with a basic form of meditation and then moved in to the essence of the method. This entailed detailing the most picturesque walled garden I could imagine. It could be a traditional garden with an orchard, vegetable plot, little fountain in the middle, and an ancient brick wall around the edge covered in centuries of ivy. It could be a futuristic fantasy garden with bees serving coffee, Christmas cake trees and cloud chairs if you wanted, but it's the details you focus on. At some point, while focused on these details, you walk to the surrounding wall and leap over it. On the other side is the answer to your question.

I know this sounds far too simple to be effective but it's a method that makes sense to me and is backed up by scientific research. (See the resources section for more information on Dr Win Wenger, or visit the above website for more answers.)

After I jumped over the wall, I was met not by a person, or a written document but by a small plant in a pot. It was swaying from side to side and I got the distinct feeling it was extremely happy. The little plant had tiny white flowers all over it and there were silver fireworks shooting out from the center of every flower.

I watched this little plant, documenting my reaction on a digital voice recorder. After I finished my session, I listened to the recording to try and determine what this display meant, if anything.

What I took from this interaction with the plant (with my original question in mind, 'what's *the* aspect of my book I should focus on?') was that while a small plant in the world view may seem inconsequential, in this encounter it had such tremendous impact, and was mesmerizing. The idea that underneath the ordinary exterior that we think we are, is really a stunning energetic glowing dance of explosive happiness.

We are such energetic beings but maybe we have smothered ourselves in so much fear and negativity that we can no longer see this mesmerizing dance in ourselves or anyone else.

I began to wonder what it would be like if we could turn a simple introduction such as between myself and this little white petaled plant, in to a one on one introduction framework between inspirer and inspired.

The point here is that we are already that, that we are seeking.

Hard to believe, right?

SELF-ESTEEM AND HOW I GOT HERE

Until very recently, I was terrified of giving speeches. If I had to give a speech at school (high school) I would practice and practice because that way I was at least able to stand up and say *something*. But my nerves would keep me awake the night before. I would have trouble eating, or thinking about anything else, and all those physical sensations would crash down upon me as I waited for my turn to speak.

At university it became easier because of the university bar. I would go there for at least two drinks before my scheduled presentation. If I timed it right, this always did the trick.

However, I was smart enough to realize that this was not a long-term solution to my fear of speaking and so I did something to deal with it. My solution, I did everything I could to avoid giving a speech in public.

ALONG CAME NANCY

In 1997 I started my Master's degree at Sheffield University in the UK. Before the course had even began I met a woman at registration called Nancy. She was studying the same course as me, and it just so happened she was very pretty as well.

It took me several weeks of getting to know Nancy before I got up the courage to ask her out, and another month to propose. This was no whirl-wind, it was a tornado.

A year later on December 1st 1998, we were married at Leez Priory, in Essex, England.

In the UK, it's customary for the groom to give a speech, thanking the bridesmaids and giving a little insight into how the bride and groom met. For three weeks before the big day, I practiced. I went up to the woods near my parent's house in Little Baddow, Essex, and practiced the crap out of my speech, lifting my voice up, shouting the words out loud just to get used to hearing my voice.

I was ready. I took no notes or cue cards. I was going to nail this speech if it was the last thing I would ever do.

The day of our wedding arrived. As the venue was built around 1550's, we wandered about with guests looking at the architecture and history and we all had a glass of champagne. If you looked at almost every picture during my wedding you would notice something, my champagne never goes down. I had a gut-wrenching nervousness that made me feel as if I had drank about 5 pints of water. I should add that this was not nervousness about getting married, but because of the speech.

I wanted to drink that champagne, trust me on this, but until we sat down for our meal and speech time, I *couldn't* drink it. One reason was, I wanted to be clear headed. This was our wedding day and I was going to act as I intended to go on.

My speech was in two halves. As I stood up, I looked out at our guests, took a deep breath and began. The first half of my speech I breezed through with no problems at all, and then I began the second half.

As I looked out at those fifty faces staring at me, something changed. I stared back and realized I had nothing. I couldn't remember a thing I had said, or what I was supposed to say next. My mind was a complete blank.

A feeling of absolute dread descended upon me. I could feel the panic beginning to rise. My knuckles turned white as I gripped the chair in front of me and after a silent, 'oh God, please help,' I reached for my last resort, my drink. If this didn't do it, I really had nothing else to give.

As my hand moved toward the glass, I heard a familiar laugh from one of our guests. It was a good friend of mine. BAM. With that laugh everything flooded back, and I lifted my head and charged forth, never faltering once.

The reason my friend laughed was because as I reached for my drink, I said in a quiet voice, '*when in doubt take a drink.*' I have no memory of saying this. My wife told me about it later.

From the time my mind went blank, to the time it all flooded back was less than two seconds. No one had noticed my fall in to hell and the desperate scramble out. As cheers and claps echoed around the room, I felt convinced my chance of delivering a fabulous wedding speech had passed me by. It was only later that I was told by friends they had never seen me so composed.

What is the point of this story?

We all have our fears, our beliefs, or lack thereof in ourselves, and no matter what those are, you know within that you are more capable, more inspiring and more powerful than you sense on the surface.

Every fear is just a past thought held on to, hiding in your subconscious. If you bring that fear into your conscious awareness, (putting yourself in the situation you fear will do it), you can let go of holding on to the thought, and the fear will dissolve. (See the resource section for more details).

We all need a bit of a faith, no matter what word or term you use, God, Jesus, Christ, Buddha, Allah, the Great Spirit, Universal Consciousness, Oneness, Love, Science, or Life, it really isn't important. What is important is that you use your faith to bring humanity back to the human race.

I think we can all agree, we are all part of the human race? Bring back this sense of Oneness but not by trying to argue your truth, or spewing anger, or belittling other's beliefs. If you can't except we are all One, part of a singular consciousness, then think of us all as Earthlings.

We have nowhere else to go after all. Each of us live on this little planet, we're born, we contribute, and in my opinion, when we leave our body, we return to being our true self, and knowing and being part of Oneness. However *you* end that sentence, we are here until we're done with these bodies, so we better find a way to get along.

If we could only accept that each of us have different beliefs about who we are, what we're doing here, how we got here, and where we're going next, we would take a quantum leap in our levels of awareness.

In *Communion With God*, Neale Donald Walsch said, '*mine is not a better way, mine is merely another way.*' If we adopted this in to our lives, do you think it would have an impact?

I think it would.

To bring this back on point, we should not be threatened by not being an expert, or not feeling inspiring enough to inspire others. Rid yourself of those thoughts. Remember, they are only thoughts *you* accepted in your past, and have held on to since.

COMPASSIONATE LISTENING.

As I see it, inspiration is a combination of two things: love and compassionate listening.

Just by listening compassionately to someone else can be inspiring to them, and possibly you. Focus on what the other person is saying. Direct them a little by asking questions that address their concerns maybe, but most of us already have the answers to our own questions. People just don't have the confidence to believe that they have them.

By listening compassionately, meaning, don't check the internet on your phone, or look at the clock every few minutes. In fact, turn off your phone, put it out of sight, and bless them with your undivided, focused attention. You can inspire someone by making them the center of attention because they *are* that important. Help them to feel that within. By doing just this, they are far more likely to find answers and attribute their success to you, whether you want it or not.

The 'Now'

Another area to focus on with regard to compassionate listening is that 'Now' moment and how to stay in it. I go in to this in more detail in chapter two, but it's so enriching that I wanted to mention it here. The Now is something we have gotten out the habit of being in. Focusing on the Now moment is so incredibly life altering, that it's worth putting in the effort.

If you use the Now method described in chapter two while listening to someone, you will have more clarity and feel mesmerized by what they're saying. This will help you and encourage them.

It is worth practicing this beforehand as it takes a little getting used to.

Inspiration is Something You Give Away

Life has become so much about 'getting more stuff'. We have been fooled into believing that stuff equates to success, but this 'stuff' is merely filler.

What do I mean by that?

When we buy a new toy, whether a car, house, jewelry, a DVD, a book, course or whatever, we get a buzz. We're lifted from wherever we are, temporarily. After a while however, we lose that great buzz and find ourselves back where we were, and often beating ourselves up about buying the thing in the first place. So, what do we do? We buy something else. We are basically creating a buzz to fill the void.

But what if the void wasn't really there? What if this void was only your desperate want of happiness, a want of love?

I believe, beneath all the negativity we've accumulated over our lives, is our true all loving self. We just can't feel it, depending on the depth of our negative garbage above.

> *"ANYTIME ONE FEELS GOOD, ONE IS LOVING. ANYTIME ONE FEELS BAD, ONE IS NOT LOVING."*
> LESTER LEVENSON

According to Neale Donald Walsch in 'Conversations with God', Book 4, *"the fastest way to awaken more quickly is to be the cause of someone else awakening more quickly."* This is one of the points I am trying to make in this book. I'm not only wanting to present that idea to you and show you the evidence why your inspiration *is* needed, but also to prove to you that you *Can* inspire others, change their lives and change your life by doing so.

This is the concept of doing something for someone else, without wanting anything in return.

I'm sure you have questions about the whole *awakening* process, but that is a whole other topic and could easily take up an entire book on its own. If you want to research the awakening process further, I have mentioned several great books on the subject in the resources section.

What if Someone Doesn't Get It?

What if a person you are sitting down with is unimpressed by your efforts to inspire them, or feel they are beyond help? Then what do you do?

You will certainly come up against people who think you are wasting your time trying to make a difference in their lives. They will likely dismiss the idea you *can* help, or say that you don't have the experience to do so. It happens. What is important to understand is, you are not necessarily going to announce to someone that you are there to inspire them. Why say, *"hey, I'm going to inspire you to do great things, to follow the path you've always dreamt of being on?"*

As I said earlier, you can just sit and listen, as if that person is your oldest friend talking to you. Don't act all bubbly, pushing them in a direction they are not comfortable with, no matter how inspiring it sounds. Be yourself. Take it slowly.

You are a guide fighting your way through a thick jungle, moving and cutting vines and vegetation out of the way to show there is a path *to* follow. I'm sure many people would like to go at it with a bulldozer but this rarely if ever works out well for anyone.

Being Careful Where You Tread

It *is* important to be aware of other people's beliefs.

People are passionate about their beliefs. We have this sense that what we believe is right and if only everyone else could get on board, they would be much happier. As someone trying to help and inspire, you are not there to alter or change another person's views on the world. Your goal should be to steer them along a path and inspire them to believe that they *can* do it. If their beliefs change while doing this, fine, but that's not why you are there.

There is no need to push your beliefs on someone else to inspire them, no matter what they believe. As with everyone, they have as much right to believe whatever they like and hold it to their hearts as you or I do with our beliefs.

I am also not suggesting you follow what *I* believe. My core values are set out as an example of what I think goes on, that's all. Use what feels right to you as *your* guide.

What I'm saying in this book is what I believe. I am saying, 'Here is another way.' It's not the only way, and I am not the first one to suggest it.

The same message can be written down in book format over the centuries by different authors, and some will understand the message while others will not. It may take the one hundredth writer to put that message a slightly different way for one person *to* get it. If I can get just one or two people to get it, and go out there to inspire change, I will deem this a success.

EVERYTHING AND NOTHING

I have read book after book on Chinese medicine, meridians, qigong, and martial arts. It's a fascinating subject, but when it came to the idea of the Tao, or 'the way of being' in traditional Chinese medicine I was lost. Where things got complicated for me was how we could be both *everything and nothing*, as suggested by Lao Tzu in the Tao de Ching. At the time, this went over my head. I couldn't adjust to this way of thinking. It wasn't until I began reading books by Lester Levenson and listening to his seminars that I got it.

Now, when I say I got it, I don't mean I was suddenly free, or enlightened, or a realized being. Far from it. I, like most, am burdened with the weight of my past thinking, but the wonderful thing is, I had found a way to lighten my load, to unburden myself of my self-imposed limitations if I chose to.

That is what I return to every day when I am feeling down, or lost, or fragile, the idea that whatever is going on around me, whether illness, frustration with my work, my family, or worry about where I'm heading next, was created by my thinking in the past. What I am holding on to still, is what is molding my future circumstances and situations to come.

At that moment, I can sit back and think, because this is my creation, by changing how I think now, my world next week, or next month will change. It may not be dramatic. It's best to work on one thing at a time until completion, but even small steps lead to the finish line in a marathon.

We have all been presented with a magnificent opportunity to reach beyond ourselves to inspire, to influence, to guide and teach. It is in our hands how the world turns out. It is our responsibility to make the changes necessary for global impact. We can make this impact one person at a time. Only we *can* do it.

"WHEN YOU ARE INSPIRED BY SOME GREAT PURPOSE, SOME EXTRAORDINARY PROJECT, ALL OF YOUR THOUGHTS BREAK THEIR BONDS: YOUR MIND TRANSCENDS LIMITATIONS, YOUR CONSCIOUSNESS EXPANDS IN EVERY DIRECTION AND YOU FIND YOURSELF IN A NEW, GREAT AND WONDERFUL WORLD. DORMANT FORCES, FACULTIES AND TALENTS BECOME ALIVE AND YOU DISCOVER YOURSELF TO BE A GREATER PERSON THAN YOU EVER DREAMED YOURSELF TO BE."
ROBIN SHARMA

SUMMARY

You can do this because I can do this. I had never felt like someone who could inspire others to make their lives better than they were. I was always so shy, and such an introvert. But that is what's so great about all this because you do not need to be an inspiration, or Captain Inspire, the one who stood out at school and everyone wanted to be them. This is about being the authentic you, it's about compassionate listening, being interested, and putting your immediate desires aside, just for a short time, and focus on someone else.

Inspiration is a gift you give away without wanting anything in return.

The idea of inspiring someone else can be scary, but if you look at it this way, it will make all the difference.

Imagine you are sitting down with your oldest friend whom you haven't seen in years. <u>It's a conversation</u>. Have a conversation and include genuine interest, compassionate listening and a little encouragement here and there. You will do wonders just from this.

Don't be afraid of failing because failure doesn't exist. "*I never fail. I either win, or I learn*" Nelson Mandela. If your efforts to inspire someone come up short, learn from it, don't beat yourself up.

We are amazing energetic beings but because of the way we have structured society, we can't help but be smothered in fear and negativity from the moment we wake up to when we go to sleep. It can be a challenge to get underneath the ordinary exterior we think we are, and see how stunning, mesmerizing and extra-ordinary we really are. So try to think of yourself as such. Imagine spreading love and warmth to everyone you come in contact with.

In the following chapter 'Living through your heart,' we will explore how being heart centered can help guide you and give you clarity when faced with stressful situations

MY SEVENTH CHALLENGE TO YOU

With all the talk of inspiring and guiding others to follow their path, it seems appropriate to begin doing just that. So, I challenge you to sit down with someone you know well, a family member, or a friend. Get them to open up about what they want to achieve, no matter how large or small. Listen to what they have to say and guide them when you feel it appropriate to do so.

That's all.

This is a lesson in listening. The object of this challenge is to prove to you that by just listening compassionately you can do this. Some of you may find this is a real challenge. Your focus may flit about like something crazy. You might suddenly realize you have no idea what they have been say-ing for the last minute. This is okay. It happens to us all. But the more you do this, the more you will find your focus. If you just try and do this challenge every now and then even with the same person it will help you later.

CHAPTER THREE

LIVING THROUGH YOUR HEART

*A*ccording to research from the HeartMath Institute in California, *"the heart's electrical field is about sixty times greater in amplitude than the electrical activity generated by the brain... Furthermore, the magnetic field produced by the heart is more than five thousand times greater in strength than the field generated by the brain and can be detected a number of feet away from the body, in all directions."*

WHY IS THIS IMPORTANT FOR INSPIRING OTHERS?

We *feel* in our heart, emotions flooding out along with the physical changes that go with them. For instance, when we get nervous, we feel our heart pounding, our mouth dries up, sometimes our mind goes blank and our hands shake uncontrollably. All this can affect us and those around us. Becoming nervous when about to stand up to give a presentation is not so much our mind's creation but our heart's reaction to the environment we're in, based on past thinking and past reactions to a similar situation. Our mind then backs up those stimuli with suggestions such as, '*I can't do this,*' '*Are you crazy, remember what happened last time,*' '*Oh my God, I'm going to die.*'

When we sit down with someone, they pick up on those signals, just as we pick up their signals.

When you go for an interview for a job, you sit there in the lobby outside the office, your heart begins to pound louder as you wait. The energy signals you give off can decide your fate almost the second you walk in the room, even before you've said a word. You sense how you've done in that interview well *before* the official word.

INSPIRATION AND INTUITION

What has intuition got to do with inspiration? When I was researching this chapter, I asked myself the same thing. I did this because my purpose with each chapter was to draw the reader a picture of what is possible. I wanted you to realize the potential in every moment of our lives and pass that on to those you inspire.

I felt far too many of us give in to mainstream thinking and programming. We don't question enough. We accept things purely if said by a doctor, or scientist, or even a friend or acquaintance. Within intuition is a source of understanding that resonates somewhere other than the mind. I believe the heart has input in this process.

I called this chapter 'living through the heart' because the heart

> *"THERE IS A UNIVERSAL, INTELLIGENT, LIFE FORCE THAT EXISTS WITHIN EVERYONE AND EVERYTHING. IT RESIDES WITHIN EACH ONE OF US AS A DEEP WISDOM, AN INNER KNOWING. WE CAN ACCESS THIS WONDERFUL SOURCE OF KNOWLEDGE AND WISDOM THROUGH OUR INTUITION, AN INNER SENSE THAT TELLS US WHAT FEELS RIGHT AND TRUE FOR US AT ANY GIVEN MOMENT."*
> SHAKTI GAWAIN

provides that connection to something much larger than the physical bodies we call ourselves. The heart is far more important than we give it credit. It is more than just a pump.

SO WHAT ELSE *IS* THE HEART? LET'S GO DOWN THE RABBIT HOLE

Don't be freaked out, we're not going full on Mad Hatter here. Simply put, our mind is the accumulation of all our past thinking. Whether it's information gleaned from reading a book, or magazine, or article, a thought popping up while watching a movie, or from just listening to what is said around us while ordering a coffee, our emotional thought response to it can affect our future. Of all the past accumulation of thoughts, the thoughts we hold in mind, the ones we keep coming back to all the time create the world around us.

So why, you may be asking, don't I have all those things I've thought about? The mansion by the beach with a fortune in diamonds in a secret safe, the Aston Martin DB5, the luxury holiday penthouse in Zurich, or the private jet. We'll come to that later. But just to say, whatever you think you've been thinking of, is not what you've held in mind.

How does this relate to our intuition and inspiring others?

First, our intuition is not the mind. It is something else and somewhere else. When we hear our intuition, it's not so much a thought from the mind but a sense of some kind, possibly from the heart.

Recent studies by the HeartMath Institute have shown that the brain, while powerful, unique and mysterious, is not necessarily the seat of power within us. The heart has an innate intelligence. It's not just a pump. *"The heart has a complex neural*

*network that is sufficiently extensive to be character-
ized as a brain on the heart."*

What the HeartMath Institute found was,
when a person is shown an image that generates an
emotional response, it is not the brain that reacts
first but the heart. *"The heart in particular seemed
to have its own logic that frequently diverged from
the direction of autonomic nervous system activity.
The heart was behaving as though it had a mind
of its own. Furthermore, the heart appeared to be
sending meaningful messages to the brain that the
brain not only understood, but also obeyed. Even
more intriguing was that it looked as though these
messages could affect a person's perceptions, behavior
and performance."*

The heart reacts first, sending a signal to the
brain to tell *it* how to react, and the brain follows
these survival instructions accordingly.

What happens therefore when our intuition
pops up and tries to direct us?

Our past thinking jumps in to play, giving us
a past response to a similar situation and we act
on that. The intuition is shut down because of
this response. It is shut down because our mind
is far too noisy to allow the initial intuitive heart
thought to get through all the junk.

When we hear our intuitive heart thought,
it is because our mind is quiet. We might be just
spacing at the time, or so focused on one question
going around our mind that most other thoughts

are silenced, so the intuitive answer slips through for us to hear it.

Can I prove this as fact? No, it is a theory but the evidence we have, such as that from the Heartmath Institute, supports the theory.

Intuition can jump out at any time, for any reason. I lived in Alaska for several years in the early 2000's. My wife and I were members of the Oriental Healing Arts Center in Anchorage where we studied and practiced Tai Chi, qigong, and meditation. On one occasion, we went to an open house seminar given by our instructors held in an auditorium in downtown Anchorage. There were maybe sixty people present. As we sat there listening, I was feeling very calm and peaceful. Somewhere during the latter proceedings, they started to announce door prizes.

If you remember, at that time in my life I had a real fear of talking in public, or getting up on stage in public, that kind of thing.

The first prize was tai chi lessons which I wanted to win. I didn't. They announced the winner and he got up onstage to receive his prize. Then they said, 'and the second prize is a massage,' and picked up the hat with everyone's names in it. At that moment I knew I had won that massage. This was not a wanting. I didn't want a massage. It was a knowing I had won. I began to say in my head, 'let Nancy (my wife) win, let Nancy win.' *And the winner is…..*" I won, and was asked to go up on stage to collect my massage coupon. Let me say that again, this was not me thinking, 'maybe I will win,' or, 'I have already won,' or even, 'I will win,' it was a foregone conclusion, I knew I had won.

Apart from the fear of getting up on stage to collect my prize, I felt like a Jedi master, just one with fear, *'these aren't the droids you're looking for'* kind of thing. I think the reason I had this insight was because my mind was so clear of clutter at that moment that the intuitive thought had room to maneuver and make its presence known.

Why is this story of my intuitive sense so important?

I believe I allowed myself that insight into winning the massage for a reason.

First, I believe I brought this 'win' to me, on a subconscious level because I needed it. The reason for that is, several weeks after this event, I badly injured my back at work. I was an archaeologist working on Fort Richardson in Anchorage. My back swelled up, I had shooting pains going up it as if someone was poking me with an electric cattle prod. It was the most painful experience of my life. I was informed by the physical therapist that my back muscles were extremely tight and maybe I focus all my stress on my lower back. She recommended massages and muscle strengthening exercises. And of course, I had won a massage. That could have helped.

Well, I may have won that massage, but I didn't use it. I gave it to my wife. I often wonder if my intuition was making a direct call saying to me, *'you need a massage, you're too tight, too stressed, here it is.'*

Intuition is not an essential element to inspiring someone, but by moving into the space where your intuition resides and can function effectively, you will find a sense of clarity, peace and an awareness most dismiss or allow to pass unacknowledged. By being more attentive and in tune with your intuitive powers, you will find it much easier to not only deliver inspiration, but also, you will exhibit a sense of trustworthiness within you.

My main desire when inspiring someone is to inspire them to push past their fears, not to let deep seated or even minor fears stop them achieving. I use the example of public speaking in this book only because my fear of it had such an effect on me over the years. I believe with encouragement and someone to inspire me, I would have overcome that fear and made the leap to being a competent and relatively fearless public speaker much faster.

The whole concept of inspiration is not to take the person you inspire all the way to their goal, whether big or small, but to inspire them to that point where they can do it on their own.

So, don't feel overwhelmed if a friend says their goal is to summit Mount Everest when they have issues climbing the stairs in their house. You are there to get them on the path and move them enough where they can see the path and are energized to follow it.

You do not need to go full on mountaineer and train for those heights unless it's something that is also your passion, but don't seek out only those challenges you are passionate about. Allow your intuition, your gut response to lead you if you can.

Now that's quite a statement to make; follow your gut response. How on earth do we do that? Isn't intuition something that pops up here and there as a subtle and questionable guide?

What if we could live every moment of our lives based purely on our intuition? I can hear you saying, I don't believe it.

BRANSON INTUITION

Sir Richard Branson is certainly someone most people have heard of. He is an entrepreneur extraordinaire. He is also one of the few mega entrepreneurs to admit his business decision making has been strongly influenced by his intuition. Is he always right? No. Branson has had his failures just like all successful people, but it doesn't stop him from listening.

BELIEF AND KNOWING

Intuition is our true selves trying to guide us, but we get in our own way. This is what I believe, and I don't think I'm living in crazy town.

I look for answers in some peculiar places admittedly, but I always look to verify using whatever scientific principles I can because that is how we currently think. Until we have that evidence, there is always a lack of true belief.

I believe for instance, when I look out at the stars at night that there are millions of other species living around the universe. There is no doubt in my mind. However, although I would love to believe we currently share a base on the moon with alien beings, whenever I say, *I believe there's a base on the moon that we share with aliens from another world,* I know I don't fully believe it. I may *want* to believe it, but the belief is lacking. Until I see photographic, scientific, verified research to prove it, there will always be that doubt in my mind.

When we sense our intuitive response to something, it is an all-knowing feeling. We know it's right, at least for a fraction of a second before our past thinking jumps out and kicks it aside. Sometimes however, we can keep our minds quiet and hear our intuition, then listen to it and act.

"IF PRAYER IS YOU TALKING TO GOD, THEN INTUITION IS GOD TALKING TO YOU."
DR WAYNE DYER

SUMMARY

In society, we have always focused on our heart as the pump. Just an organ to push blood around the body. Yes, it does this, and does it very well, but it does so much more. It is *not* just a pump.

We feel from our heart. Can you remember a time when someone you cared about gave you a hug or a kiss? You probably felt different within yourself. A warmth, a wave of love or happiness. Where did that feeling come from? It came from within you. It came from your heart. You didn't think about how to feel, or what to feel. It was a physical feeling, that brought on an emotional response.

Your intuition is another fabulous tool in life's tool bag that we tend to disregard and ignore. It is constantly trying to get through to you with subconscious messages. By allowing access to your intuitive powers, you are engaging in a conversation with the universe. This is an incredibly powerful tool, if you listen. We all have our intuition pinging away all the time trying to get our attention. The more we listen and acknowledge this inner power, the louder it will become, the clearer it will be. Think of the impact this can have in your life and in the lives of those you look to inspire.

In the following chapter 'That Divine Spark', we will experiment with the Now moment and experience the peace that is the divine. If you follow the steps outlined in the next chapter, your life really can transform very easily. But to achieve it, you must commit to doing it, and not just once.

MY EIGHTH CHALLENGE TO YOU

This challenge is an exercise in quiet. It requires being in a place where you will not be disturbed. The television, stereo, or phone have been turned off. Anyone living in your home is aware what you are doing and gives you the time to do it. You want to be at peace with yourself.

I challenge you to find your place. Get comfortable. Make sure you are wearing comfortable clothing, nothing tight or restrictive. Close your eyes and begin to focus on your breathing.

Whenever a thought pops into your head (which it will), just bring your attention back to your breathing.

Really try and focus on your in breath. Hear the sound and feel of it. Do the same with your out breath. This will become easier with practice. Continue to do this every day for fifteen or twenty minutes to begin with.

Don't stress yourself out thinking it must be done perfectly.

Don't beat yourself up because you had a million thoughts pour out while doing this. It happens, we have become programmed to live that way.

Most of those thoughts are irrelevant to improving your life. Just bring your awareness back to your breathing every time a thought pops up. It *will* take time to adopt a new pattern, but when you do, a whole other world has opened up to you. It has been there all along, it's just the amount of thoughts pouring from our minds has obscured the conversation.

Your intuition is probably *not* going to jump in and start handing you the secrets of the universe however. This is a learning experience. The more you do it, the more the fog will be lifted, opening you up to your intuitive potential. There are so many benefits to this practice, but I want you to focus on just clarity of thought for the time being.

CHAPTER TWO

THAT DIVINE SPARK

I BELIEVE WE ALL HAVE A PURPOSE FOR BEING HERE

I do not accept the typical life story of, I'm here to learn, work, make as much money as I can, buy nice stuff and die. It doesn't make sense to me and I think if you're still reading this book, then it doesn't jibe with you either.

So why *are* we here?

This is a question with no right or wrong answer. We all have an opinion. Why should one opinion be better than any other, right?

My core values in Chapter five give you a pretty good idea what I believe and how I think reality works, but for the record, here is *my* opinion.

It's a question we all think we have an opinion on until we're asked what it is, then everything seems to dry up, we stutter, cough and realize we're not so sure after all.

It can take years to identify what you really believe based not on what you are told by others, but what you feel is right in your heart. I believe whole heartedly that we are all connected to oneness. That there is no separation between anything. How I treat you, is how I treat myself. What I do to you, I do to myself. We are here to experience this divine oneness while in our 'separated' physical form. To overcome the fears and lack of connectedness we see all around our little planet every day and feel divine unconditional love for everyone.

I'm not asking that you except my opinion. In fact, I would be amazed if you did. There may be similarities here and there but really, you should be using how you feel about life as the fuel to make a difference.

We are all influenced somewhat by what others say, and how they say it. You might find something I have said connects with you, alters your view of everything, makes the journey you are on less bumpy, or provides a little clarity. If so, that's great but that's not the primary purpose here.

LIVE IN THE MOMENT

The concept of living in the moment is both obvious to most people but totally alien to them at the same time. Of course we live now, right now, how else could we live? But we do not *consciously* live there.

Most of us decide to live in our memories, which are the past, and our fears and desires, which are the future. We rarely give the present moment a second's thought.

So let's do an **E**xperiment. It is very similar to your eighth challenge but there is a subtle difference.

The idea with this experiment is to try and be present in this moment.

Close your eyes, focus on your breathing. Breath in and breath out. Now, while focusing on your breathe begin to say to yourself either aloud or in your head, '*Now, Now, Now,*' and keep focusing on '*Now.*' It's very simple to be in the now, but I wonder how long you can stay there?

Finding the now moment and getting used to staying there for a time can really help when it comes to listening compassionately to others. After all, they're telling you something about themselves that is incredibly important to them. What you may find when sitting there with a person you are hoping to inspire is that your mind flits from what they're saying, to whatever your mind throws out there. How often have you found yourself doing this? I used to do it all the time. I had what was known as a 'monkey mind' or active imagination.

It can be tough to stay focused when you're sitting and listening to someone, especially if the subject is not in your area of interest to begin with. This is where all the practice of being in the now moment can help.

To Hear, You Must Get Quiet

The divine is the quietness that you hear and the peace you feel when you move in to the now moment. If you stop and be in the now, I believe you hear God. Everything else just drops away, your fears, concerns, worries, hates, negativities they all disappear until you realize you are quiet.

At that moment you think again, thoughts re-emerge. But instead of becoming frustrated, use these intrusions as your guide. Each time you have a thought and recognize it as such, move back to the Now moment. This becomes easier the more you do it.

One of the best explanations of the 'Now' and how to be in it, is given by Eckhart Tolle in his book, 'The Power of Now.'

"Instead of "watching the thinker," you can also create a gap in the mind stream simply by directing the focus of your attention into the Now. Just become intensely conscious of the present moment. This is a deeply satisfying thing to do. In this way, you draw consciousness away from the mind activity and create a gap of no-mind in which you are highly alert and aware but not thinking. This is the essence of meditation.

In your everyday life, you can practice this by taking any routine activity that normally is only a means to an end and giving it your fullest attention, so that it becomes an end in itself. For example, every time you walk up and down the stairs in your house or place of work, pay close attention to every step, every movement, even your breathing. Be totally present. Or when you wash your hands, pay attention to all the sense perceptions associated with the activity: the sound and feel of the water, the movement of your hands, the scent of the soap, and so on. Or when you get into your car, after you close the door, pause for a few seconds and observe the flow of your breath. Become aware of a silent but powerful sense of presence. There is one certain criterion by which you can measure your success in this practice: the degree of peace that you feel within."

I was reminded of the importance of being in the Now moment recently when my eight year son asked me, '*why is it that a year has only twelve months which isn't very long, but it takes so long to get to Christmas?*'

Do you remember when you were in 3rd grade and the school day lasted forever? It seems like yesterday to me.

When my son asked me that question, I looked at him and realized he was bored. He was sitting there fidgeting, looking fed up, thinking of how far away Christmas morning was and all the presents. His focus was almost entirely on future events, his desires.

Sometimes, talking to a young child (especially one who is in the 'Why?' stage) can clarify your thoughts because you have to. There is no option if you want to be understood.

This is what I told him.

Hans, we have so many exciting things to happen before Christmas. There's parties, decorating the Christmas tree, hanging the lights, singing in your Christmas play, stirring the Christmas pudding, (I'm English, and he loves Christmas pudding). All these things and so much more are happening before Christmas morning.

Do you see that by focusing your attention on if you're going to get what you want at Christmas, you might miss what's happening in each magical moment before Christmas? The future is what you want for Christmas, the past is what you got last Christmas, and all the other Christmases before that, but you are living 'Now.' Don't miss all the wonderful things happening in this moment because all of a sudden, it *will* be Christmas day and you would have missed all the magic leading up to it.

I would love to think he got the message I was trying to show him. He listened, then said, '*Oh okay, but why does it take so long to get to Christmas when there are only twelve months in a year?*' It made sense to me but may not have made any sense to him.

This Is What This Message Comes Down To

Simplify, as if you were talking to a child. That is what I hope I have accomplished with this book. I want everyone who picks up this book to have a clear understanding of the message by the time they put it down. I'm not trying to be smart with the things I'm writing here, I just want it to be as clear as glass.

It's clear to me but is it clear to you?

To inspire clarity, we need dialogue. With this in mind, your ninth challenge will directly connect us.

SUMMARY

Why are we here? It's the trillion dollar question. Is it to learn, to find what interests us and work in that area? Is it to earn enough money to buy a nice house and car, to eat in great restaurants with someone who tugs at our heart strings? I don't think it is, but what do you think? What do you feel?

There is no right answer. It's all about what *feels* right to you, what *you* believe to be the answer. However, the concept of it all being about getting more stuff just doesn't resonate with me. I believe we are all connected and therefore how we treat and act towards one another cannot be over looked. We're talking about oneness, karma, and living in the now moment.

To hear the voice of God, or your intuition, or the great spirit, or your subconscious, you must get your mind quiet. You must allow your thoughts to float by like clouds on a windy day. (For further information see the Resources section).

In the following and final chapter 'What is danger? It's not doing what you love', we are going to ask why people do not do what they love when they have the power right in their hands to live a life of love and happiness?

MY NINTH CHALLENGE TO YOU

My website (www.yi-in.com) gives you and I the opportunity to connect. It is where we can challenge each other through experience and dialogue to forward the message written about here. I intend to put forward correspondence via written articles, video blog and sections from this book to connect to people.

I want to know what you think and feel about all this, and the journey you have been on while reading this.

My challenge to you therefore, is to write how you feel about this process. Let me know what you need (if anything) to make this work better or easier.

Document your experiences in your Gain Journal and offer your observations as an on-going collaboration. This is important as it will develop a fluid stream of thought between us and anyone else on this journey.

All the greatest accomplishments the world has ever known started with a simple conversation. Let's talk and see if we can change the world.

CHAPTER ONE

WHAT IS DANGER?
IT'S NOT DOING WHAT YOU LOVE

ARE YOU LISTENING?

The understanding that it's from within that all power comes, is, as stated earlier, not a new one. It has been around for thousands of years, taught by enlightened masters of the past, yet we have suppressed it, dismissed it and mostly ignored it to our cost.

After all that time of having the power to make our impact on the world, to make a difference for all humankind right in our hands, it is only now the message might finally be getting through. That might be because things have got so bad that we are actively looking for answers. We are now at the cusp of change, but change is not guaranteed.

The question we must ask is, will we turn our backs on this incredible power once again?

We're sitting on the treasure mounds of the universe bemoaning our lack while staring off in to the distance.

How have we continually missed this amazing opportunity after all these years being taught about it and how to use it? We have been acting like the high schooler in the 'Secrets of the Universe' class, ignoring the lesson to tell our friends what a great part time job we have lined up. '*Ten bucks an hour dude, that's how much I'll earn.*'

This brings to mind an analogy: "*A young man once picked up a sovereign lying in the road. Ever afterward, walking along, he kept his eye fixed steadily upon the ground in hopes to find another. And in the course of a long life he did pick, at different times, a goodly number of coins, gold and silver. But all these years, while he was looking for them, he saw not, that the heavens were bright above him, and nature beautiful around. He never once allowed his eyes to look up from the mud and filth in which he sought his treasure; and when he died – a rich old man- he only knew this fair earth as a dirty road to pick up money as you walk along.*" John Bate.

It's time we stopped searching for pennies and begin to explore where the treasure really lies. It's time we embraced the Oneness we are, that all who live on this planet are.

By treating others the way we wish to be treated, inspiring and empowering them to new heights, we are inspiring and empowering ourselves and lifting our existence to where we can be and should be.

Become the change you so desperately want to see in the world… Allow any fears you may have of this experience and process to come up, then change them into a wonderous, exciting and inspired adventure. Allow your fears to empower you.

DO WHAT YOU LOVE

Doing what you love may seem like an obvious statement. Doesn't everyone follow their interests and do what they love?

I don't think so.

Most of us follow a path laid out with the least bumps and the straightest route that leads to a good or great salary. Sometimes interest follows along but I think for most, it's a distant second at best.

LEAD BY EXAMPLE

I have tried to follow my passions. Every six or seven years, I find myself at a fork in the road. When this occurs, I have a decision to make:

Follow the path I'm on, or veer off on to a new untrodden path.

It's not the easiest decision to make as I have a family and responsibilities, but I also have a voice within urging to push the boundaries no matter what. You do not need to do everything all at once however. One step at a time is all it takes. Og Mandino challenged us when he said, "*I will be liken to the rain drop which washes away the mountain; the ant who devours a tiger; the star which brightens the earth; the slave who builds a pyramid. I will build my castle one brick at a time for I know that small attempts, repeated, will complete any undertaking… I will persist until I succeed.*"

As I stated earlier in the book, even small steps complete a marathon eventually.

I started out as an Archaeologist, then went in to the field of physical anthropology, and from there followed the path to disaster management. Each of these new areas connected with the last without a problem. Then I came to a new fork. On this occasion I followed the path untraveled. A whole new career, new tools, new courses and new adventures. It was exciting and frightening all at once. My new career was as a freelance writer.

Leading by example is a life style. It is not something done on occasion.

MY FIRST EXAMPLE

How can you use the information in this book to inspire?

One of my first more successful attempts to inspire someone occurred without realizing it. It was a chat with a friend about a business idea he was interested in. This was the spark that lead to writing a book on business mindset with him, but at the time I just wanted to help him and see what he wanted to accomplish. I was simply listening.

Where I felt I could offer advice, I did. Where I felt he needed to think along new avenues, I suggested it. We sat and broke his dream in to small bite sized parts and wrote it all down as we went. That was it.

Whenever we have met I have asked about his dream, not to keep account but to show I'm still interested. This has always led to a detailed conversation about what he needs to do next, and how to get to that next step or platform. I enjoy the process and it shows.

Above all else, you should enjoy the time you have inspiring others.

WHAT HAPPENS NEXT? THE MYSTERY OF NOT KNOWING

Some of you may know the legend of the *Mary Celeste*.

On November 7th 1872, the brigantine '*Mary Celeste*' set sail from Staten Island on her way to Genoa with 10 passengers and crew. Ten days after she left port, she was found floating abandoned off the Azores in the Atlantic. Her sails were partially set, and she looked disheveled but sea worthy. There were 6 months of food in her stores, and her cargo was intact. There was three and half feet of water in her hold which was not excessive for a ship in those days. Her only life boat was missing. The passengers and crew were never heard of or seen again.

We still do not fully understand what happened to the *Mary Celeste* or to her crew and passengers, but as this example shows, do not wait for things to happen because you don't know how long you've got. Is that a little morbid? Maybe. My point is, make sure to put your heart and soul into whatever you are wanting to accomplish. Make it happen with intent, commitment and action.

As in the above example we can never know what *is* going to happen next in our lives. In every moment, everything in our lives can change, and not necessarily in a bad way. Every moment of our lives has fabulous potential and glorious opportunity waiting around every corner. Rabbi Shoni Labowitz, wrote in his book, 'Miraculous Living,' *'every moment is a miracle unfolding,'* and he was absolutely right. It just depends on how you look at it.

So what's going to happen next in your life?

What miracle is about to unfold in your life?

You could potentially help bring about a miracle in someone else's life.

"Close your eyes and you will see clearly.

Cease to listen and you will hear truth.

Be silent and your heart will sing.

Seek no contacts and you will find union.

Be still and you will move forward- on the tide of the spirit.

Be gentle and you will need no strength.

Be patient and you will achieve all things.

Be humble and you will remain entire.

Stop thinking and you will end problems."

A Taoist meditation-

> *"DON'T GIVE UP. THERE ARE TOO MANY NAY-SAYERS OUT THERE WHO WILL TRY TO DISCOURAGE YOU. DON'T LISTEN TO THEM. THE ONLY ONE WHO CAN MAKE YOU GIVE UP IS YOURSELF."*
> - SIDNEY SHELDON

Follow your heart. Isn't it from your heart that you feel love? Isn't it from your heart you feel warmth and happiness? If you follow the wisdom in your heart, you will always win. No matter what goes on around you, you will always win.

SUMMARY

All power comes from within you. It has always been there. Whatever is brought to your attention, use it as a guide to free the negativities within you.

If you use this, you will find life responding, but get an understanding of this before using it to inspire others.

Follow your heart.

Lead by example. Be an example to your family. Be an example at work. Be an example to the stranger on the street. It's not that hard. It is about living through your heart, loving what you do, and enjoying every moment of it.

In the 'Resources' section I have listed the books, courses, techniques and methods that have influenced me the most. I have no affiliate links to any of them and do not profit by you investigating them and potentially buying their books or courses. I am merely expressing what I feel they are about and what I have gained from applying the information they present.

I look forward to hearing about your adventures on your journey.

MY TENTH CHALLENGE TO YOU

This is the last challenge for you. It's not so much an exercise but a hope.

My challenge for you is to push past any lingering doubts you may have, (express them on the website if you have them) and begin this journey of inspiration.

If you haven't already taken that first step, just begin small. Talk with a family member or friend about what it is that inspires them. What do they want to achieve?

Remember, even the smallest spark can ignite a forest of dreams. That's all it takes, one spark. That spark is getting someone to believe in themselves. We all have incredible potential within us. We are all capable of magnificent and life changing decisions. We have within us the power to make a difference. Sometimes all we need is a little push.

What difference will you make in the world?

ACKNOWLEDGEMENTS

While researching this book I delved deep into the world of releasing, matrix energetics, meditation, qigong, and the fears we are surrounded by. It was a wonderful and soul touching adventure.

Many people assisted me in my quest, much of the time through encouragement and clear thinking. I needed this more than I expected. My wife Nancy was a tornado of encouragement. Almost every week she would push me to move further than I thought I could, but also provided the clarity to continue. She edited the book and listened to hours of content at the breakfast table to which I am forever grateful. At some point I will repay the time she spent on my goal.

Our son Hans helped by shaking the eight ball (asking his Cosmo robot) if I was on track to finish on time and doing everything I could to make it work. Most of the time I got a heads up.

The amount of fun this brought me was a source of joy when stress was building.

The Igniting Souls Tribe on Facebook provided support and encouragement when I was struggling to see the path. These authors have balanced life, writing and the understanding of author etiquette. I am proud to be a part of the group.

The people who have contributed to this book through their time, encouragement, and professional advice I thank them from my heart. I hope one day I can repay them for their support. Thank you, Jane O'Keeffe, Laura Ashford, Duncan Blount, Suzi Kennedy, Greg McIntyre, Astrid Paul, Mark Archer, Jerry McNeilly, Ron McCollum, Renee Bingham, Jay Gragg, and my parents Alan and Betty Ashford for believing in me.

RESOURCES

The Maharishi Experiment.
The Results: Taken from: (Maharishi's Program to Create World Peace: Theory and Research David W. Orme-Johnson and Michael C. Dillbeck)

The Basis of War and Terrorism: Stress in Collective Consciousness

"Maharishi identifies the source of all conflict in society as stress in the collective consciousness of the nation and the world.

The Roles of Governments and Individuals in Creating Peace
The responsibility for maintaining peace within a nation and between nations has traditionally belonged to the government. However, no government has succeeded in creating a state of inner

peace in the nation or in providing a basis for peace between nations.

Government and Collective Consciousness

The reason that governments have not succeeded in creating a peaceful world is that it is not within their power to do so. (Maharishi Mahesh Yogi, 1977, p.122).

In any nation, regardless of its system of government, the government is an innocent mirror of the collective consciousness (Maharishi Mahesh Yogi, 1977, p.122). The government can only react to whatever situation is created by the national consciousness. That is, the government itself is silently governed by the collective consciousness of the people. Whatever the quality of the collective consciousness of the nation, that too will be the quality of the government.

Thus, when there is violence in the collective consciousness, due to the accumulation of stress, then the mood and action of the government are prone to violence. In contrast, when there is coherence in the national consciousness, then peace will be the natural trend of life in the nation, and this will be reflected in the mood and actions of the government.

Thus, in order for any government to grow towards more perfect administration, growth of coherence in national consciousness is the prerequisite. (Maharishi's Program to Create World Peace, 1986)

Based on Maharishi's principles of collective consciousness, however, and as verified by the example of history, it is clear that it will not be effective to wait for governments themselves to create world peace.

Vedic literature states that "the collective consciousness of the whole universe is in one's own single awareness."

Creating Coherence in World Consciousness: The Global Maharishi Effect

"Maharishi's theory of collective consciousness predicts that it is possible to directly create an influence of coherence in any level of society, including the world as a whole," (Maharishi Mahesh Yogi, 1986, pp. 80-82) using only a "small percentage of the population identifying their awareness with the unified field." (Maharishi Mahesh Yogi, 1977).

A large body of scientific research has repeatedly confirmed the hypothesis that as few as one percent of a population practicing the TM program or an even smaller number, on the order of the square root of 1% of a population, collectively practicing the TM-Sidhi program is sufficient to produce a measurable and holistic influence of harmony and integration in the entire population (Maharishi Mahesh Yogi, 1986, p.76). This means that a group of only slightly more than

7,000 persons collectively practicing the Maharishi Technology of the Unified Field is sufficient to create an influence of peace for the whole world's population of about five billion.

As early as 1960 Maharishi predicted that when 1% of a population practices the Transcendental Meditation technique individually, then an improved quality of life would be found in the entire society. This effect was first documented at the city level in 1974,... (Borland & Landrith, 1976)... With the introduction of the advanced TM-Sidhi program... it was found that only the square root of the previous 1% figure was required to create the same influence of coherence in society when participants were practicing together in one group the Transcendental Meditation and TM-Sidhi program (Maharishi European Research University, 1979, p. 160).

The creation by a single group of a measurable influence of coherence in an entire society without interacting behaviorally with the population suggests an "action-at-a-distance" effect;

The Maharishi Effect in a War-Torn Lebanese Village

A dramatic prospective social experiment on the ability of the Maharishi Effect to reduce armed conflict was made in the Lebanese village of Baskinta, population 10,000, situated in the center of the Lebanese conflict.

Abou Nader, Alexander, and Davies (1984) studied the number of shells coming into the town, the number of people killed and wounded, and property damage in Baskinta compared with the same statistics from three control villages in the same area during a baseline period from the fall of 1978 to the spring of 1982 and during an experimental period from the summer of 1982 through the winter of 1984. The TM program was first introduced in Baskinta in May 1981 and the town reached 1% in June 1982.

As predicted, and in abrupt contrast to its previous history and to what was happening to control villages in the same area, there was a complete cessation of hostilities in Baskinta from the time 1% of its population began to practice the TM program, as measured by incoming shells, property damage, and casualties ($p<.005$ for each measure). This cessation of violence in Baskinta was in sharp contrast to the worsening trends in all the surrounding control villages.

Reduced Hostilities in the World's Trouble Spots

The research on the Ideal Society Campaign confirmed the principle that the group practice of the more advanced TM-Sidhi program by as little as the square root of 1 % of a population could improve the quality of life in society. This principle was directly tested immediately afterwards during the 10-week period from October 8 to December

23, 1978 in which a total of 1,400 experts in the TM and TM-Sidhi programs went in groups of 30 to 400 to the world's five major trouble spots. This experiment was conducted to test the hypothesis that the group practice of this technology would restore balance to the socio-political systems in those areas of the world (Orme-Johnson, Dillbeck, Bousquet, & Alexander 1979).

The teams of TM-Sidhi experts went to Rhodesia (Zimbabwe) and Zambia in the Southern Africa region, to Nicaragua and Honduras, Costa Rica, Guatemala and El Salvador in the Central America area, and to Iran, Syria, Cyprus, and Israel in the Middle East. The purpose of the groups in Israel and Cyprus was to test the hypothesis that they could mitigate the intensity of the Lebanese civil war. When these experts in the Maharishi Technology of the Unified Field went to a country, their sole activity directed towards creating peace was the twice-daily practice of the TM and TM-Sidhi programs.

An analysis of the effects of the World Peace Project on domestic affairs and international relations for these countries was conducted using the Conflict and Peace Data Bank (COPDAB), 1948-1978: Daily Aggregations (Azar, 1980; Azar & Sloan, 1975).

The COPDAB file is the largest independent daily data bank in the world coding for conflict in international affairs. The compilers of the

COPDAB file were completely independent of the World Peace Project.

The COPDAB file of international and domestic events pertaining to these countries were aggregated into three categories: (1) cooperative events; (2) verbal hostilities; and (3) hostile acts. Events were thus combined into broad, homogeneous categories in terms of degree of conflict or cooperation. During the World Peace Project the percentage of hostile actions between countries as well as between factions within the trouble spots decreased relative to the baseline period by 16.7 percentage points (from 46.4% to 29.7%). Cooperative events increased by 13.2 percentage points during the World Peace Project relative to the baseline period (from 36.0% to 49.2%, $p<.0001$).

Interestingly, verbal hostilities also increased by 3.5 percentage points, which may be interpreted as a shift from behaviorally expressed hostilities to verbal hostilities. The proportional reduction in hostile acts in these trouble-spot countries was twice as great as the proportional reduction of hostile acts in the rest of the world.

Thus, while the World Peace Project had its greatest influence on the trouble spots themselves, it also influenced the entire world."

Maharishi International University
Fairfield, Iowa, U.S.A.)

Heartmath Institute (www.heartmath.org)

Since 1992, the Heart Math Institute based in California, has been conducting experiments to test the effects of human emotion on DNA.

"HeartMath deems integral elements of the model for who we are and what we can be are the thoughts, feelings and intentions we have every day. After two decades of studies, HeartMath researchers say other factors such as the appreciation and love we have for someone or the anger and anxiety we feel also influence and can alter the outcomes of each individual's DNA blueprint." (You Can Change Your DNA July 14, 2011)

"When we are having a bad day, going through a rough period such as dealing with the sickness of a loved one or coping with financial troubles, we can actually influence our bodies – all the way down to the cellular level. But by intentionally thinking positive thoughts and focusing on positive emotions we can choose to accept whatever is showing up and have positive influence on our bodies at the same time." (Heartmath Institute)

Matrix Energetics (www.matrixenergetics.com)

Matrix Energetics is a consciousness technology developed and pioneered by Dr Richard Bartlett. *"All you might need to do, if you have a pain or a problem, is realize that your expectations are based on your perceptual bias. Your problem is always there, in part because you assume that it will be, so it shows up in the same way every time. In the next moment, it can be totally different. You assume it can't because physical reality appears to be unchanging. That is the rational assumption based on a closed-system model. It's a lie!"* P.72 The Physics of Miracles 2009 Dr Richard Bartlett.

Epigenetics (www.brucelipton.com)

The emerging scientific study of 'Epigenetics', pioneered by cellular biologist Dr Bruce Lipton, has turned medical and scientific beliefs on their head. *"We adjust our genes based on our perceptions, in fact, a mind boggling number, every gene in your body can be modified to create 30,000 different variations. From each gene... The big thing is, there's a whole history of, 'you're a victim you're a victim', and it turns out, oh my God, we were in control and we didn't know it, and because it's our perceptions that control it, whether you believe you can, or whether you believe you can't, your right... We become masters when we understand this mechanism."* ('Spontaneous Evolution.')

"If the genes control our life function, then our lives are being controlled by things outside of our ability to change them. This leads to victimization

that the illnesses and diseases that run in families are propagated through the passing of genes associated with those attributes. Laboratory evidence shows this is not true." (Genetics, Epigenetics, and Destiny. Interview with Dr. Bruce Lipton, by Danielle Graham Superconciousness Magazine. Sept 2008)

"The new science of epigenetics promises that every person on the planet has the opportunity to become who they really are, complete with unimaginable power and the ability to operate from, and go for, the highest possibilities, including healing our bodies and our culture and living in peace." Taken from: https://www.brucelipton.com/resource/article/epigenetics

The Miracle of Water

Japanese scientist Masaru Emoto wrote a book called '*The miracle of water.*' In it he describes the impact our emotions have on water by subjecting water to specific negative and positive words and emotions, then freezing the water and photographing the crystals. *"If love and gratitude retreat from the world, they will be replaced by negative vibration. In this age, the weakening of love and gratitude in one part of the world can become the cause for wars and disasters on the other side of the planet."* P.135 The Miracle of Water Masaru Emoto.

(This is evidenced in the findings of Dr David Orme-Johnson through his research *International Peace Project in the Middle East.*)

It is also valuable to remember that this world we all live on *and* our bodies are made up of 70% water. Think about the effect our thinking has on this essential element. Fear, hate, any form of negativity distorts the very physical thing we are and the thing we live on.

HOW TO ACCESS INSPIRATION?

There is always more than one way.

One reason we have not heard 'Inspiration' is because of all the noise in our minds. All the constant thoughts rushing about, most of them fear, hate, worry, stressful negative thoughts.

1- So, one way to combat this is to quiet the mind.

By quieting the mind you find a path through the garbage, your own yellow brick road directing you to the Emerald City, the universal mind, your subconscious.

2- Another way to access your inspiration is to use a technique or method called releasing, or letting go.

There are a number of great companies at the forefront of the releasing movement:

The Release Technique (Thereleasetechnique.com)
The Sedona Method (Sedona.com)
KISS Releasing (kissreleasingsystem.com)
The Power of Quiet (powerofquiet.com)

They all work, the difference between them is the personality of the instruction. It just depends on which personality suits you best.

3- Another access point to the limitless power of the subconscious is from a scientist and visionary Dr Win Wenger. He has a technique called 'Image Streaming' which I have found very effective in getting the conscious mind distracted enough to allow access to the infinite power of your inner mind. (winwenger.com)

4- One other consciousness technology that I will mention is from Dr Richard Bartlett. He developed Matrix Energetics. Again, this is very effective and fun to do if you grasp the implications of it. If you do, you will find a whole new world opening up. (matrixenergetics.com)

5- The books of Robert Collier (The Secret of the Ages, Riches within your Reach), Charles Haanel (The Master Key System, The Amazing Secrets of the Yogi), and Arjuna Ardagh (The Translucent Revolution).

REFERENCES

Dedication - Lester Levenson – The Ultimate Truth About Love and Happiness – 2003

Epigraph - Robin Sharma – The Monk Who Sold his Ferrari - 1999

CHAPTER 10

Tony Robbins – '11 Things You Didn't Know About the Superstar Life Coach' By Nicole Sawyer and Rebecca Jarvis. Mar 10, 2015 Abcnews.go.com

Neale Donald Walsch – Conversations with God Book 4 2017

Mark Twight – Extreme Alpinism 1999

CHAPTER 9

Neale Donald Walsch – The Storm before the Calm 2011 P.43

Michael Talbot – The Holographic Universe 1991 P.41

Neale Donald Walsch – What God Said 2013

Robert Christiansen & Greg McIntyre – Rockstar Lawyer 2017

Dr Bruce Lipton – Initiating global evolution: The Science of Emergence 2.55-3.38 YouTube

Edgar Cayce – Reading# 792-2

Eckhart Tolle – The Power of Now 2004 P.25.

CHAPTER 8

Dr Bruce Lipton – Happy Thoughts = Happy Life. Conversations with Robyn Walker.

Dr Bruce Lipton – The Biology of Belief 2016

Michael Talbot – The Holographic Universe 1991

CHAPTER 7

Lester Levenson – Keys to the Ultimate Freedom 1993 Ch.1

Burt Goldman – The Mind Box part 1, 2007

Eckhart Tolle – The Power of Now 2004

Robert Collier – The Secret of the Ages 1926 Vol.1

William Makepeace Thackeray – Vanity Fair

Gregg Braden – The Divine Matrix 2008 P.6

Eckhart **T**olle – 'Dealing with Anger, Resistance and Pessimism.' YouTube

Dr **D**avid **O**rme-**J**ohnson – The Journal of Conflict Resolution, International Peace Project in the Middle East.

Gene **R**oddenberry – Star Trek The Motion Picture 1979 p.221

Arjuna **A**rdagh – The Translucent Revolution 2005

Dr **B**ruce Lipton – The Biology of Belief 2016

CHAPTER 6

Betty **S**mith – A Tree Grows in Brooklyn

Dr **R**ichard **B**artlett – The Physics of Miracles 2010 p.101

Ralph **W**aldo Emerson –

CHAPTER 5

Maltbie **D**avenport **B**abcock – Thoughts for Every-day Living from the Spoken and Written Words of Maltbie Davenport Babcock 1901 p.29

Robert **C**ollier – Riches Within Your Reach 1947 ch.1

Win **W**enger, **Ph**.D. and **R**ichard **P**oe – The Einstein Factor A Proven New Method for Increasing Your Intelligence 1996

CHAPTER 4

Neale Donald Walsch – Communion with God 2002 ch.11

Lester Levenson – The Ultimate Truth About Love and Happiness 2003 p.10

Neale Donald Walsch – Conversations with God Book 4 Awaken the Species 2017 p.5

Lao Tzu – Tao de Ching 1992

Robin Sharma – The Monk Who Sold His Ferrari 1999

CHAPTER 3

HeartMath Institute – Science of the Heart: Exploring the role of the heart in human performance 2009

Shakti Gawain – The Shakti Gawain Essentials 2015

HeartMath Institute – Science of the Heart: Exploring the role of the heart in human performance 2009

CHAPTER 2

Eckhart Tolle – The Power of Now 2004 p.17

CHAPTER 1

John Bate – Dr Jeffers A Cyclopaedia of illustrations of Moral and Religious Truths: 1865

Og **M**andino – The Greatest Salesman in the World 1983 Ch.10 Scroll III

Rabbi **S**honi **L**abowitz – Miraculous Living: A Guided Journey in Kabbalah Through the Ten Gates of the Tree of Life 1998 p.53

END QUOTE

Lester **L**evenson/ Hale Dwoskin – Happiness is Free Book.1 2001 p.169-170

ABOUT THE AUTHOR

Robert Christiansen lives in Shelby, North Carolina with his wife Nancy and their son Hans. He is originally from England. While studying a Master of Science degree in Physical Anthropology at Sheffield University in 97/98, he met his American wife Nancy who was also studying Anthropology. For him, at least, it was love at first sight. After a whirlwind month of dating, he proposed. They were married a year later and moved to the United States in 1999.

From that time on they have travelled the world, soaking in different cultures, traditions and experiences.

Robert and Nancy both worked in Bosnia with the ICMP (International Commission of Missing Persons) exhuming mass graves and analyzing the remains for identification, and in Iraq with the Regime Crimes Liaison Office exhuming mass graves and analyzing the remains for the direct prosecution of Saddam Hussein and his senior deputies.

Throughout this time Robert wrote down his experiences and adventures, but it wasn't until five years ago he turned to writing as a career.

'*Your Inspiration is Needed*' is not Robert's first book, but it is his first as a solo author and the one he most identifies with. He enjoys public speaking, getting out his comfort zone and encouraging others to do the same.

You can visit his blog at yi-in.com.

"Locked up in that word "givingness" is the key to all happiness. It's in the spirit of givingness that we have and experience the greatest joy… But it's not in the givingness; it's in the spirit of givingness that the joy lies."

Lester Levenson